POPULAR
MAP READING

POPULAR
MAP READING

By

E. D. LABORDE

ASSISTANT MASTER
AT HARROW
SCHOOL

CAMBRIDGE
AT THE UNIVERSITY PRESS
1928

CAMBRIDGE
UNIVERSITY PRESS

University Printing House, Cambridge CB2 8BS, United Kingdom

Cambridge University Press is part of the University of Cambridge.

It furthers the University's mission by disseminating knowledge in the pursuit of education, learning and research at the highest international levels of excellence.

www.cambridge.org
Information on this title: www.cambridge.org/9781107492851

© Cambridge University Press 1928

First published 1928
First paperback edition 2015

A catalogue record for this publication is available from the British Library

ISBN 978-1-107-49285-1 Paperback

CONTENTS

ILLUSTRATIONS

DIAGRAMS

ILLUSTRATIONS

MAPS

In addition to Maps III, VI, VII, and Fig. 7, on which special acknowledgments to H.M. Stationery Office appear, Maps I, II, IV, and V, and Figs. 18, 19, 20, 21, 23, 24, 25, 26, 27, 28, 29, 36, 41, 44, 47, 48 *a*, 54, 55, 56, and 57 are based upon the Ordnance Survey Map, with the sanction of the Controller of H.M. Stationery Office. Fig. 48 *b* is from a photograph by Valentine and Sons. Fig. 50 is reproduced by kind permission of Messrs J. H. Steward, Ltd.

FOREWORD

The following chapters represent an elaboration of the writer's notes compiled for use with his divisions at Harrow and treat the subject in a simple manner.

The aim has been to produce a popular work, a text-book which the non-specialist can appreciate, and above all one that is not too unpleasant to read. The map is introduced from the very beginning and is kept in the forefront throughout. There is a minimum of mathematics, and what there is has been put simply and in a way likely to appeal to those whose forte is not mathematics. Topographical features are described and illustrated, and their representations on the map are given as standards of reference. A map area is discussed at length and the method of combining separate features to form a whole landscape is fully treated. Last and perhaps most important of all, the human interest is kept in view throughout, and the uses of Map Reading to the geographer, the rambler, the mountaineer, the motorist, the soldier or the historian are urged in the hope of bringing the subject into touch with the living world. Whether these aims and methods have been successful or not the reader will judge.

No examination purposes have been envisaged in writing the book, but by coincidence the first two chapters exactly cover the requirements of the Oxford and Cambridge Joint Board's School Certificate Examination. The many schools that restrict their Map Reading to the syllabus of the A Certificate of the War Office will find all they require in sections 1–9, 12, 14–15, 17–18. Those who are not too closely fettered by examinations will find, it is hoped, that the scheme may be adapted to their Geography schedules. But it is also hoped that the book will commend itself to those who are not at school and who find a knowledge of Map Reading necessary or desirable.

In conclusion, the writer's best thanks are due to his pupils at Harrow for their aid in trying out methods, to his colleague, Mr Maurice Clarke, for the admirable block diagrams which he has so kindly contributed, and to Mr Walter Lewis and Mr G. V. Carey, of the Cambridge University Press, for the trouble they have taken over the production of the book.

                                                    E.D.L.

HARROW-ON-THE-HILL
    October, 1928

INTRODUCTION

A map is a representation of the whole or a part of the Earth's surface. It is not a picture, since it does not show objects in perspective, but in proportionate size, and because it represents its area in plan. The reasons for these differences are obvious. Perspective emphasises near objects at the expense of more distant ones, while in side views, as in pictures, elevated objects hide from the eye whatever lies behind them. The fact that objects are shown in plan must be borne in mind, for by it all distances which are not perfectly horizontal are more or less foreshortened and consequently all areas not in a horizontal plane are shown in some degree smaller than they really are (see Fig. 1).

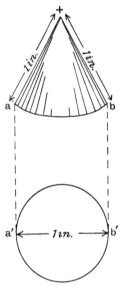

Fig. 1. Projection in plan of a hill.

Not only does the map show the ground from this unusual point of view, but it also shows the whole subject in reduced size. It is evident that but for this reduction, the map would have to be as big as the area represented. Hence, to show the area on a sheet of reasonable size, every part of it must be proportionately reduced. In some cases this procedure would reduce objects to an invisible point; so, in order that they may be seen, they are represented by signs large enough to be noticed (see below, sect. 5).

These characteristics make a map a conventional drawing and its interpretation an art. The skilful map reader is able to form from careful study of the map a good idea of the appearance of the country. But, to become skilful, constant practice with the map is necessary, and the imagination must be brought into play.

There are various kinds of maps, all intended for special purposes. The kind with which it is proposed to deal here is the topographical map, that is, one which shows minor features of the land relief. The chief topographical map of the British Isles is the one-inch map of the Ordnance Survey, on the Popular Edition of which the treatment in these pages will be based.

This map is produced by the Ordnance Survey, a department set up by the British Government in 1791 to compile a map of Great Britain. In the early maps relief was not shown, but after 1860 hill features were represented by various devices which will be dealt with later. The mapping of the country has long since been completed, but the results are constantly being revised and brought up to date. Generally speaking, the one-inch map is revised every 15 years, various areas being dealt with successively. But corrections, such as the insertion of new roads and railways, are made more frequently.

For convenience' sake the map is issued in numbered sheets, there being one series for Scotland and another for England and Wales. There are 92 sheets in the former series and 146 in the latter. An index on the cover or in the margin of each sheet shows the numbers of adjacent sheets.

CHAPTER I

PRELIMINARY

1. THE MARGIN AND THE FRAME OF THE MAP

The Margin. On looking at a sheet of the Ordnance Survey one-inch Popular map, one sees a wide margin surrounding it. In this margin will be found:

(i) An index of the adjacent sheets,
(ii) the date up to which the sheet has been revised and corrected,
(iii) the direction of True and Magnetic North,
(iv) a scale of distances, and
(v) the height of the vertical interval.

The purpose of the first of these notes is obvious and has been referred to already. The importance of the date of last revision and correction is apt to be overlooked, however, unless it is realised that certain features, e.g. woods, buildings, etc., vary with time, and that therefore the older the map the less likely it is to be accurate in these matters. The meaning and use of the other three notes will be explained later in the proper place.

The Frame. Inside the margin is printed a narrow frame in which are shown:

(i) The latitude and longitude,
(ii) parts of place names which overflow from one sheet to another,
(iii) the destination of roads leading off the sheet, and
(iv) certain letters and figures which will be explained in the next section.

The indication of latitude and longitude is of little importance to the topographical reader, but the completion of place names and the note on the destination of roads are an obvious convenience.

2. The Squares

Turning to the map itself, one notices that it is covered with a network of lines dividing the surface into squares. As each pair of parallel lines is separated by an interval of two inches, the length of each side of the squares is two inches. Hence, each square represents an area of four square miles. Each space between lines running east and west is indicated by a letter (shown in the map frame), the topmost space being A, the next below B, and so on. Similarly, the spaces between north-and-south lines are indicated by numbers, the left-hand space being 1, the next on its right being 2, and so on.

These squares have three important uses: the indication of position, the judging and indication of direction, and the judging of distance.

Indication of Position. When the position of a place is to be communicated to a person or group of persons, as, for instance, a class or an assembly of officers, by another person who cannot indicate the point in question by a touch of the finger, the latter need only name the square in which the feature occurs and the feature itself. This narrows down the field of search. Thus, to find X, situated in square H7, as only one square occurs in both space H and space 7, X must lie in that square. Once the square is found the feature can usually be located.

Sometimes, however, the feature is not prominent, has no name, or is one of several similar features on the same square. In such cases, the position of the feature can be indicated in one of the following ways:

(i) By naming a point of reference which is easily found and then by stating the direction of the feature from that point. E.g. 'H7; find the village of X. Due east is a windmill'.

(ii) By using the letters in prominent place names in the following way: 'H10; find the corner of the wood just south of the <u>h</u> in Northolt'.

(iii) By using a system of coordinates, in which the sides of the square named are imagined to be divided into ten equal parts, as in Fig. 2. The south-western corner of the square is taken as zero and the divisions numbered consecutively from one to nine. To describe the position of a point *P*, the eastward divisions are reckoned first, and then the northward. The position of *P* is then described as G2—34 (read as 'G two—three four', since the figures have no numerical significance). This is naturally the most accurate method.[1]

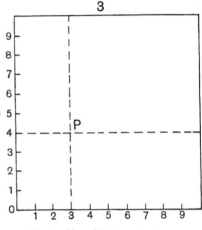

Fig. 2. Use of map squares.

Judging and Indication of Direction. As the square lines run due north and south, or due east and west, their presence assists the eye in judging direction, whether in observing or in indicating the position of places.

Judging Distance. Since the square lines are all two inches apart, they help the eye to judge the distance from one point to another.

Exercises on Map References

(References are to Map III)

1. Square A2, find Wendover, Upper Icknield Way.
2. Square B2; find Smalldean Farm. To the west is an inn.
3. Square B2; find the point on the main road at the first ɲ in Little London.
4. Find the following points: B2—23; C3—64; A2—33; A2—39.

[1] The military grid system secures even greater accuracy. It is described on p. 97.

5. Using each method in turn, describe the positions of Great Missenden, Lee, and Little Hampden.

6. Using a suitable method, describe the positions of Dunsmore, Scrubs, Moat Farm.

7. In what way is Question 6 a practical illustration of the use of map squares for the indication of position?

3. BEARINGS

There are many ways of indicating the direction of a point from a known position, but the method commonly used by map readers is to give an angular measurement known as a bearing. The nature of a bearing and the method of measuring it will best be understood from a diagram. In Fig. 3 let P be the point of reference. With P as centre and any convenient radius, describe a circle. Draw the radius PN. Imagine the circle to be graduated like a protractor, with the degrees numbered in a clockwise direction from PN right round the circle. Now, a straight line joining P and any point A cuts the graduations at (say) C. The angle NPA, whose measurement in degrees may be read at C, is the bearing of A from P. Mark P and A on the figure, draw the straight line PA, and measure the angle NPA.

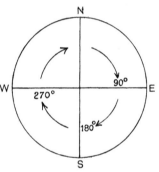

Fig. 3. Measurement of bearings.

N, it should be noted, is north of P, and PN is a north-and-south line. Hence, a bearing is an angular measurement from the north taken in a clockwise direction.

Exercises

1. Take a point P on a north-and-south line PN. Assuming N to be north of P, draw straight lines from P showing the direction of places with bearings of 25°, 32°, 108°, 143°, 289°, 330°, respectively from P. (N.B. This process is known as *laying off a bearing*.)

2. Let *PN* be a north-and-south line with *P* south of *N*. Lay off bearings of 90°, 180°, 270°, respectively from *P*. What names are commonly given to these directions?

3. In the accompanying figure, find the bearings of *A*, *B*, *C*, *D*, and *E* from *P*.

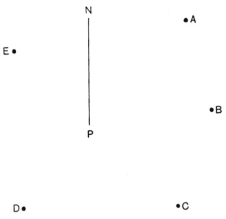

Fig. 4. Exercise on finding bearings.

In taking bearings off a map there is the practical difficulty that there is no north-and-south line drawn through the point of reference. For rough purposes the north may be guessed, but for accurate work a north-and-south line is necessary. Here it may be noted that the lines of the map squares run north and south or east and west. Consequently, a north-and-south line may be drawn through the point of reference by making the line parallel to the nearest north-and-south line of the network.

But the best method is to join the point of reference and the objective by a straight line and produce this, if necessary, to cut a north-and-south square-line, as in Fig. 5. Thus, to find the bearing of *A* from *P*: *SL* is the square-line and *AZ* the production of *PA*, cutting *SL* at *C*. Then the angle *SCZ* is the required bearing.

This may be proved geometrically by drawing through *P* a straight line *NR* parallel to *SL*. Since *NR* and *SL* are parallel and

PZ is a straight line cutting them, $\angle NPZ = \angle SCZ$. And since $\angle NPZ$ is the bearing of *A* from *P*, $\angle SCZ$ also gives the required bearing.

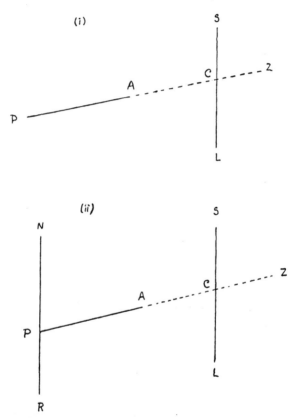

Fig. 5. Measurement of a bearing from map squares.

Once the principle is understood, it will be possible to work from the east-and-west square-lines as well as from the north-and-south.

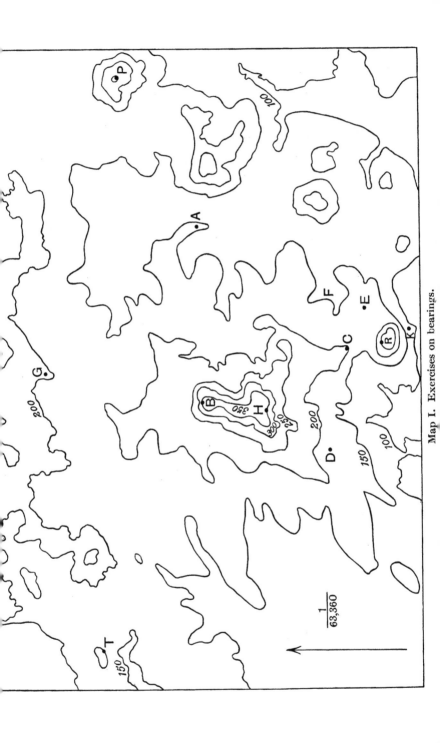

Map I. Exercises on bearings.

Exercises on Map I

1. From *B* find the bearings of *G, A, E, D.*
2. Find the bearing of *B* from *G, A, E, D.*
3. Find the bearings of *G, B, C* from *P.*
4. Find the bearing of *P* from *G, B, C.*
5. Through *D* draw a straight line running due east and west and with its help find the bearing of *R.*
6. The bearing of *P* from *A* is 61°. Join *AP* and with the help of this line draw a north-and-south line through *A.*
7. The bearing of *TB* is 113°. Join *TB* and with the help of this line draw a north-and-south line through *T* and one through *B.*

4. MEASUREMENT OF DISTANCE

The shortest distance between any two points on a map can easily be measured with a ruler. The actual distance on the ground may

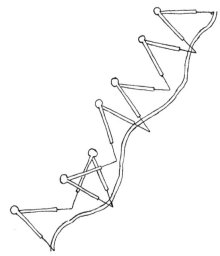

Fig. 6. Measurement of a curved road.

then be calculated. By the scale, 1 in. on the map represents 1 mile on the ground; hence, 3 in. on the map represent 3 miles; 4·5 in. on the map represent $4\frac{1}{2}$ miles, and so on.

But usually the distances to be measured on a map are not straight. It is more useful, for instance, to know the distance by road or rail between two towns than it is to know the distance 'as the crow flies'. There are various ways of measuring distance along a curved line, but the following are suggested as practical and simple:

(i) Divide the curved line into a number of short sections and measure each section as in Fig. 6. Then add up their lengths. A rapid form of this method is to step the distance with dividers (see Fig. 6). The result is only approximate.

(ii) Lay a piece of fine thread along the line to be measured in such a way that the thread follows all the curves of the line. Carefully mark on the thread, by knots or otherwise, the beginning and end of the measurement. Straighten out the thread and measure the distance along a ruler. This method gives far more accurate results, but needs practice.

(iii) Instrument makers sell a practical little meter made on the same principle as a cyclometer. With its aid distances may be measured quickly along curved or straight lines. It is well, however, not to rely on instruments which may not always be available.

Exercises on the Measurement of Distance

1. On Map I measure the following distances 'as the crow flies' and say what distances they represent on the ground: *B* to *A*, *G*, and *T*; *H* to *P*, *R*, and *T*.

2. What are the lengths of the sides of Map I? What is the area of the ground shown on the map?

3. Shade the ground enclosed on the central hill in Map I by the 350-foot contour. What is its greatest length? and its average breadth? What is its area?

4. On Map III measure the length of the Upper Icknield Way; of the Lower Icknield Way. Give both the length on the map and the distance on the ground.

5. How far is it by road from the church at Prestwood (Map III, C2) to Great Missenden station?

6. Which is the greater distance and by how much: from Hampden Bottom (Map III, C2) to Bottom Farm, or from the same starting point to the road junction at Little Hampden?

5. CONVENTIONAL SIGNS

It has been pointed out already that certain objects are too small to be shown in their proportionate size on a one-inch map and that they must therefore be indicated by means of pre-arranged symbols. Such objects are post offices, wind pumps, buoys, etc. But there are others, like woods, which, though big enough to be shown proportionately, yet require some symbol to indicate their character. Hence, the map reader must learn to recognise a large number of signs and to know their meaning. Most of these are given in the margin of the map sheet, but this should not tempt the reader to rely on the key, for the reading of the map would be a slow and painful business if the meaning of the signs had to be constantly looked up.

The signs are easily learnt. They are either simple conventional pictures suggesting the objects they represent, e.g. windmills, wind pumps, etc.; or they may be colour patches standing for such things as woods, rivers, etc.; or else they may be initial letters of the names of the objects, e.g. T for post and telegraph office. An important form of conventional sign is the use of different type for different kinds of objects. Thus, ranges of hills and other important physical features are distinguished by one kind of type; single peaks and minor features by another. Towns are graded and their grade indicated by the type used. Antiquities are shown in type which denotes their period. Thus, the names of Roman remains are written in 'Egyptian' characters; e.g. **ROMAN CAMP**; and the names of remains of all other periods in 'Old English' characters; e.g. 𝔊𝔯𝔦𝔪𝔰' 𝔇𝔶𝔨𝔢.

Exercises on Conventional Signs

1. Make a list of the conventional signs, classifying them under the heads (a) conventional pictures, (b) initials, (c) colour patches, and (d) simple marks.

2. Draw the signs for church with tower, church with spire, church with neither tower nor spire, windmill, wind pump, lighthouse, lightship.

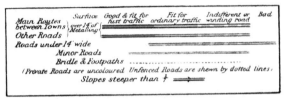

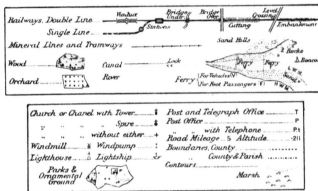

Fig. 7. The Characteristic Sheet of an O.S. Popular map.

Reproduced from the Ordnance Survey Map with the sanction of H.M. Stationery Office.

3. How are coniferous trees distinguished from deciduous on the map? Draw small woods showing both types.

4. How are orchards and parks distinguished from woods?

5. Draw a section of railway line showing how double lines are distinguished from single, and illustrating the symbols for cutting, embankment, level crossing, bridge under, bridge over, and station.

6. What signs represent a tramway, a marsh, sandhills, sand, a county boundary?

7. What is the meaning of H.W.M. and L.W.M.?

8. What is the difference between Ferry V and Ferry F?

9. Draw enlarged signs for embankment, cutting, lock, beacon, church with tower, viaduct.

10. What is the meaning of the signs: T, P, P.t, 5, ·382?

11. How are roads with slopes steeper than 1/7 distinguished?

12. What are the four classes of roads? Into what sub-classes are they divided?

13. How are unfenced roads distinguished?

14. Draw examples of 'main routes good and fit for fast traffic', 'other roads indifferent', minor road, and footpath.

(N.B. *The following questions refer to* Map III)

15. You are staying at Great Missenden. Where would you go for a walk, using footpaths and avoiding roads as far as possible?

16. Your car has broken down at Bottom Farm (B1). What is the nearest telegraph office?

17. Is the railway between Great Missenden and Wendover double or single lined? Find an embankment, a cutting, a bridge over, a bridge under.

(N.B. *The following are drawing exercises*)

18. Draw a sketch map of an imaginary village with post and telegraph office, a church with spire, and an inn. A main route passes through it and an 'other road' crosses the main route in the village.

19. Make a sketch map showing two villages five miles apart and connected by a branch road and a single-line railway. There is an embankment a mile away from one village and a cutting two miles from the other. Make the road cross the railway once by a bridge over, once by a bridge under. Insert in each village a post and telegraph office, a station, a church, an inn.

20. A village stands on the banks of a stream. A road runs north through the village crossing the stream by a bridge. Above the bridge is a lock and two miles down stream is a ferry for foot passengers which is attached to a branch road. A mile from the village is a country house with an orchard and a park. Show these facts in a sketch map.

CHAPTER II

TOPOGRAPHICAL FEATURES, THEIR REPRE-
SENTATION, RECOGNITION, AND
DESCRIPTION

6. FEATURES AND THEIR DETAIL

The surface of land is either high as compared with the surrounding country, or else it is low. In the former case the relief is positive, in the latter negative. Hills, mountains, ridges, plateaux, etc., belong to the first class; valleys, plains, and hollows to the second.

(a) Positive Relief

The Hill. The commonest form of positive relief is the hill, i.e. a relatively small area of high ground in which the surface falls away on all sides. It has four characteristic parts: the foot, the brow, the crest, and the summit. The *foot* of a hill is the line along

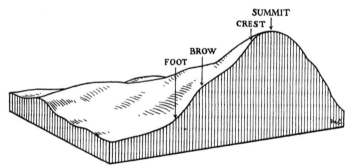

Fig. 8. The parts of a hill.

which the steeper slope of the high ground changes to the gentler incline of the valley or plain. The line is more or less definitely marked according to the nature of the slope. It has a human importance in that it is often the upper limit of cultivation and springs not uncommonly rise near it. As a rule it is not chosen as a house spot, because it is liable to be damp and is exposed to the rush of water or rock down the hill, if the slope is steep.

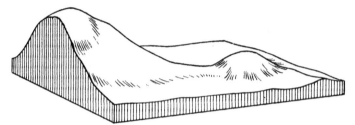

Fig. 9. A spur ending in a foothill.

When the general slope of a hill is convex, the line along which the slope becomes steeper is known as the *brow*. This is of great importance in military operations, since it commands the lower slope and the plain below. It is sometimes known as the *military*

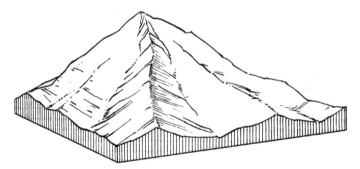

Fig. 10. A peak with buttresses.

or *apparent crest*. It is often chosen as a house site by people of means on account of its outlook and the comparatively level ground above it. If the hill is fairly high, the brow is frequently wooded. Most hills have a line near the top at which a gentle upper slope changes to a longer and steeper lower slope. This line is the real *crest* of the hill. It is not however the *summit*, or highest point.

Most hills have one or more incidental parts. The commonest of these is a projection of high ground termed generally a *spur*. Spurs which are comparatively short are known as *shoulders* or *buttresses*. Some spurs do not descend regularly, but after a time rise again to form a *foothill*. Where a buttress or any other form of spur ends in a broad, precipitous slope, the feature is known as a *bluff*. A projecting mass of rock on the side or on the top of a hill is a *crag*, unless it is small and slender, when the term *pinnacle* is preferred.

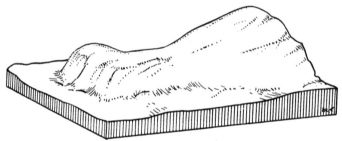

Fig. 11. A spur ending in a bluff.

Hills are classified according to their size. A lofty hill is called a *mountain*, but the distinction between a hill and a mountain is indefinite and varies with different countries. In the British Isles the mountains of the north and west seldom rise above 2000 or 3000 ft. But in regions of high relief, the term hill is applied to far loftier elevations than these. A massive hill of irregular shape and having more than one peak is described as a *massif* or *hill mass*. The English term is the better one, since the French equivalent is also used to denote a horst. A low detached hill is known as a *hillock*. A still lower elevation of the same kind is a *knoll*, while a slight elevation of whatever shape is often termed a *rise*.

Historical reasons have led to the use of local terms for hills in various parts of the British Isles, and these appear in names on the O.S. map. Thus, in the north the word *fell* frequently occurs (Shapfell, Carter Fell, etc.). In the north midlands *low* is met with, while in Devonshire *tor* is used to denote the hills characteristic of that county. Besides these there are certain prefixes which are of more or less local occurrence. Thus, the Welsh *pen* (Pen y gent), *carn* (Carn Bodvean), and the Scotch *cairn* (Cairngorm). The suffix *don* is more universal and occurs in the names of such widely separated places as Maldon, London, Snowdon.

The Ridge. A *ridge* is a long strip of high ground usually connecting two greater elevations. Hence, the part of a spur connecting a foothill to the main hill is a ridge. The characteristic parts of a ridge

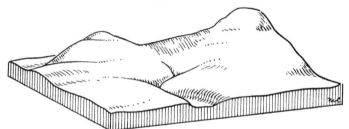

Fig. 12. A ridge connecting two hills.

correspond to those of the hill. Thus, the foot of a ridge is identical in definition with the foot of a hill. Brows do not often occur, but there is usually a crest. The most important part of a ridge, however, is the line of highest ground, termed the *ridge-line*, which corresponds to the summit of a hill.

Ridges are classified and named according to their shape. If the ridge is short, lofty, and steep-sided, it forms a *col*; if low and broad, it is a *saddle*.

Ranges. A series of hills or mountains with their connecting ridges is termed a *range*. A low ridge in a range is termed a *pass* and is of great human importance as affording comparatively easy communication between the lowlands on either side of the mountains. A road usually threads the pass, and a town lies at its foot, either as a development of a strategic military post or as the outcome of the concentration of routes on the pass. A pass which has been lowered by the action of running water is termed a *gap*. Long narrow passes are *defiles*.

Sometimes a range of hills, like the Chilterns, presents a gentle slope in one direction, while in the other it offers a steep face. The latter is known as an *escarpment*.

Plateaux. The term escarpment is given, however, to any long and comparatively regular steep slope. Such slopes are often found on one face of *plateaux*. This feature is an area of high and relatively level ground which falls away on at least one side. A series of plateaux rising one above the other like steps form *terraces*. Often a section of an escarpment is detached by erosion from the main elevation and becomes an *outlier*. The outliers of the Rhine valley are often crowned by a castle, the inaccessible lair from which the medieval robber-baron sallied forth to prey upon the plain below.

(b) Negative Relief

The Plain. This feature is of no great importance in topography, since it is usually too big in area for narrow topographical treatment. It may be defined as an expanse of comparatively level ground. Small upland plains sometimes occur in the silted up basins of former lakes. They are necessarily of great fertility, and occur here and there in Wales and Scotland.

The Hollow. This is a vague term for ground lying below its surroundings. A hollow is not necessarily enclosed. If it is, there is usually water in it forming a *lake*. A special type of small mountain lake thought to have been caused by glacial action is known as a *tarn*. Other lakes of long outline, parallel sides, and great depth, which are also at least partly due to glacial action in former times, are the *lochs* of Scotland. In England a term found in names and used especially in the east is *mere* (Windermere), though the name *broad* is used locally in Norfolk. Small artificial lakes are termed *ponds*. In districts formed of limestone or other soluble rock, dry hollows are numerous and bear local names.

The Valley. The chief negative feature is the *valley*. It is the most important of all topographical features, as it is the centre of man's activities and the nurse of civilisation. Hence, its parts have been carefully distinguished and named. It is a trench lying between

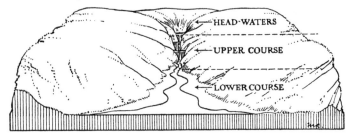

Fig. 13. The parts of a river: (i) the head-waters or collecting basin, (ii) the upper course with waterfalls and other irregularities, and (iii) the slow, meandering lower course.

two elevations. It has four essential parts: the head, the mouth, the floor, and the valley-line. The *head* is the upper end and is usually high up among the hills. The *floor* is the bottom of the valley and is bounded at the sides by the foot of the encircling hills. It slopes away from the head down to the *mouth*, which is the lower end of the valley. The *valley-line* is the line of lowest ground running lengthways down the slope of the floor. Like the ridge-line it is of great topographical importance.

Valleys may be divided into main and branch valleys. The former have their mouths on the sea and are often very large. The latter are smaller and open into a main valley. But the terms are relative, and a branch valley is often called a main valley in relation to a sub-branch valley which opens into it.

Valleys may also be classified according to their shape. The chief type is the **V**-shaped valley, in which the ground slopes gradually down on both sides to the valley-line. Such valleys are generally due to erosion by running water. Special varieties of

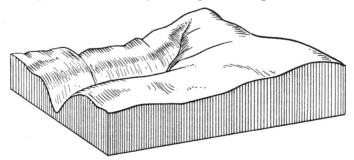

Fig. 14 *a*. A V-shaped valley.

the type, whose distinguishing features are due to geological formation or some local physical agent, occur in certain districts and bear local names. Thus, a small, deep-cut valley with a steep valley-line is generally termed a *ravine* or *gully*. In the south-west of

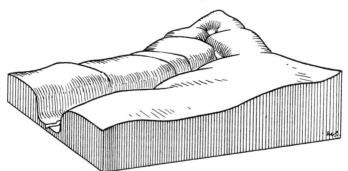

Fig. 14 *b*. A U-shaped valley. Note the flat bottom, steep sides, and flattish shoulders. The head-waters rise in a corrie.

England it is called a *chine*. In Wales and Devonshire a small steep-sided valley is known as a *coomb*, while in Scotland a similar, though usually larger, feature is called a *glen*.

Another type of valley is U-shaped. This occurs in countries which have been glaciated and is due to glacial erosion. It is in fact an old glacier bed. Hence, it has precipitous parallel sides and a flat floor. It occurs frequently in Scotland, where a small variety goes under the local name of *corrie*. This is not parallel-sided, but basin-shaped, since it was the old catchment basin, or *cirque*, of a glacier.

The River. With valleys are associated rivers, and every valley-line is an actual or potential watercourse. The head of the valley forms the *catchment basin* of the stream and is shaped like half a wash basin. When it rains, the water rushes down the sides of the catchment basin into the *channel*. Often there is a spring at the foot of the slope, and this forms the *source* of the river. Other catchment basins lie on both sides of the one just described, and the whole series together form the *head-waters* of the river. Their channels unite to form the *upper course*, a part of the stream which is distinguished by the irregularity of its slope and consequently by the occurrence of rapids, falls, and cataracts. The stream is constantly being joined by *tributaries* which rush down the sides of the main valley, bringing vast quantities of sediment and piling it up at the junction with the main stream. This sediment is laid down in a more or less triangular shape and is known as an *alluvial fan*. It is of some importance, as its fertility usually causes the growth of a village at its apex. The formation of the fan pushes the main stream over to the far side of the valley.

As the valley-line of a river is on the whole concave, in spite of local exceptions, after a time the river reaches its *lower* course, where the slope is less steep. Hence, much sediment is deposited, and the river tends to wind about in its own alluvium, forming *meanders*. An abandoned meander sometimes survives as a *mort-lake*. On reaching the sea or lake the river sometimes deposits sediment at its mouth, thus giving rise to a *delta*. At other times, there is a broad *estuary*, whose *limit of navigation* is of considerable importance and is usually the site of a port. *Mud flats* or *sand spits* often lie in or near the mouth of the river. Their occurrence depends on the local action of the tides.

Fig. 15. View of a river basin. Note the ridge forming the water-parting, the mortlake, the flood plain, and the deltaic islands at the mouth.

In some valleys and plains the slope is so gentle as to check the run off of surface water and a *swamp* or *marsh* is formed. An extensive area of swamp is known as a *morass* or *fen*.

Topographical Lines

Two of the lines mentioned above are of the highest importance in topography, viz. the ridge-line and the valley-line. The latter is always marked out by streams, which show at a glance on the map the trend of the lower ground. Even on the ground they are useful guides, and the exploration of new countries, like America and Africa, has always begun by following the big rivers.

The ridge-line, when continued over the summits of hills, marks the axis of the high ground. As the surface slopes down on both sides, the water drains off in opposite directions. Hence, the line forms the *waterparting* between streams. It follows from this that the basin, or area drained by a stream, is bounded by a ridge-line. The term waterparting is usually restricted, however, to the ridge-line which separates the basins of two main streams. The main waterparting which separates the basins of rivers emptying into one branch of the ocean from those of other rivers is termed a *divide*. E.g. the Pennines form a divide in the north of England. Thus, the surface of a district is divided into a number of areas, each of which is indicated by a river and its tributaries and bounded by a ridge-line.

Exercises

1. Explain what is meant by positive and negative relief.
2. What is a hill? How does a hill differ from a mountain? Define and illustrate with a diagram the four parts of a hill.
3. Define *knoll, buttress, pinnacle, bluff, hillock.*
4. What are: an *escarpment*, an *outlier*?
5. What is the human importance of a pass?
6. Mention any local names you know which denote hills. How have they come into use?
7. Describe what is meant by a ridge-line. How does it differ from a waterparting and a divide?
8. Define *col, alluvial fan, pond, saddle, mortlake, meander.*
9. What is a lake? What local names for varieties of lakes do you know? Where are they used?
10. State what are the essential parts of a valley and describe each.
11. Give two ways of classifying valleys and describe the classes obtained in each case.
12. Mention any local names you know denoting special varieties of valleys. Describe the variety in each case.
13. What are the three parts of a river? Describe each.
14. What are the main topographical lines? Account for their importance.

Note. The learner is advised to observe the topographical features in his own district and to find as many of the types mentioned above as he can. Practice on the ground is of extreme importance in map reading.

7. Representation of Features on the Map

It must now be shown how topographical features are represented on the map. Differences of level are shown on the O.S. one-inch Popular map entirely by means of *contours*, i.e. lines drawn through places of equal height above sea level. By sea level is meant, as far as Ordnance Survey maps are concerned, the mean height of the sea between high and low water mark at Liverpool[1]. The shore-line contour is supposed to continue this height round the coast and to mark the line of separation between the sea and the land. Higher ground is shown by a series of other contour lines drawn at intervals of 50 ft. above sea level. Thus, the rise in vertical height between any two contours is 50 ft. This is known as the *vertical interval* (V.I.) and is of the greatest importance in reading the map. As was pointed out above, the height of the V.I. is noted in the margin of the map. This is necessary, for the V.I. varies in different maps. In the O.S. six-inch map, for instance, the V.I. is 100 ft.

Fig. 16 will help the beginner to understand the principle of contours. It shows a block diagram of a hill with part of one side carved away, leaving a vertical wall. The face of the wall has been graduated to show height in feet above sea level. The graduation lines are naturally at equal intervals apart, but they do not divide the slope of the hill into equal portions. When the slope is gentle, the portions are greater than on a steeper incline. Thus, in the figure the distance between the contours for 350 and 400 ft. is less than that between the contours for 300 and 350 ft. The difference becomes still more striking if the points at which the graduation lines cut the slope are projected on the base line, as of course

---

[1] This starting point for the measurement of height is known as the O.S. Datum. In the new levelling, begun in 1912 and finished as to its framework in 1921, Liverpool being in enclosed waters was given up as a datum, and the new work was based on Newlyn, Cornwall, which is in the open ocean. This new levelling has not yet been incorporated in the one-inch maps.

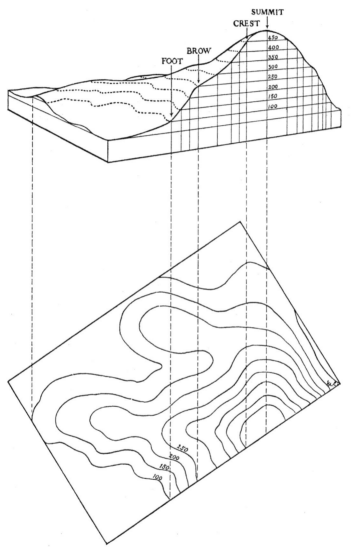

Fig. 16. The block diagram shows a hill with contours drawn on it. Note how the map below represents a projection of the contours.

they are on the map. Hence the rule that the closer together the contours the steeper the slope on the same map.

When the contours are at equal distances apart, the slope is *uniform*; when they are spaced further and further apart from the top of the hill to the bottom, the slope is *concave*; when they are closest together at some point other than the top, the slope is *convex*. Fig. 17 explains and illustrates this. These are the three main types of slope, and it is necessary for the map reader to be able to distinguish them at a glance, for, as will be seen later, many important problems arise out of their differences.

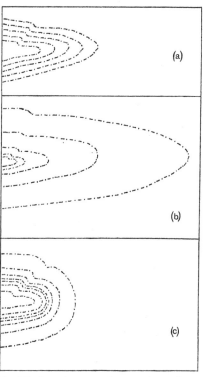

Fig. 16 gives a block diagram of a typical hill, showing summit, crest, brow, and foot. The changes of slope marking each of these is noticeable. Below is a contour system representing the same hill. It will be seen that each change of slope is indicated by a sudden increase or decrease in the spacing between the contours. Thus, after a gentle upper slope marked by a

Fig. 17. Imaginary contour systems showing (a) uniform, (b) concave, (c) convex slopes.

wide space between the summit and the 450 ft. contour, the closing up of the 400 and 450 lines shows the beginning of the steeper lower slope. Hence, the crest-line follows the 450 contour or runs

Fig. 18. A spur with foothill. Long Down Spur, Cornwall. The spur runs S.E. and is flanked by a re-entrant on either side. The ring contour near the S.E. extremity marks the foothill.

Fig. 19. A buttress. Longscale Fell. Note the buttress with its characteristic triangular points sloping away to the bottom of the figure.

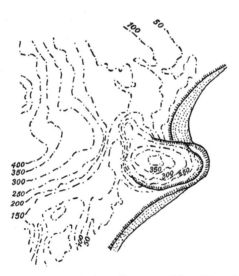

Fig. 20. A bluff. Trwyn Llanbedrog, Carnarvonshire. Note the blunt, steep salient. (This feature has the casual interest of showing a raised beach—the unshaded strip between the cliffs at the end of the bluff.)

slightly above it. Similarly, the brow may be distinguished by
the closing up of the contours, while the foot of the hill is marked
by the sudden widening out of the lines.

From the very beginning the map reader should learn to recognise contour systems at a glance and to realise without effort
what they represent. This is the ABC of map reading. Figs. 18, 19,
and 20 give the contour systems of typical incidental parts of a
hill, and Fig. 21 shows a common type of feature, the conical hill.

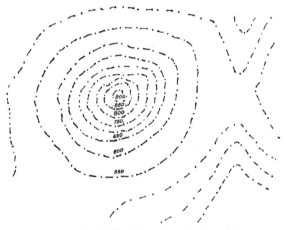

Fig. 21. A typical conical hill. After Carn Bodvean, Carnarvonshire.
Scale 2½ in. =1 mile.

Turning to negative features, it is seen in Fig. 22 that the valley
shown in the block diagram is represented by **V**-contours. Here
the height *decreases* towards the centre of the system, an important
fact which serves as an index to distinguish negative from positive
features. The valley-line is marked by the stream. It should be
observed that, since the contours which cut the valley-line are
closer together near the head of the valley than further down,
the valley-line has the normal concave slope. The ground also
slopes down on both sides obliquely to the valley-line. The foot of

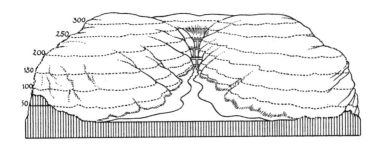

Fig. 22. The block diagram above shows a river valley with contours drawn on it. Below, the contours of the river are projected so as to form a map.

the slopes is marked by a widening out of the contours on the valley floor. The **V**-contours gradually flatten out, until the mouth of the valley is reached, where the **V** disappears.

Fig. 23 shows a complex valley with main and branch troughs. It should be noticed that the contours always push their **V**'s upstream. Figs. 24 and 25 show the two chief types of valleys which should be memorised as part of the ABC of our subject.

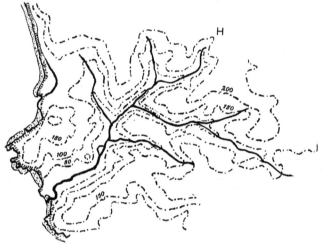

Fig. 23. A complex river valley. Gunwalloc, Cornwall. Note the branch valleys, each with its rounded catchment basin; the meanders of the lower course; and the mortlake in process of formation from a partly abandoned meander.

Fig. 26 represents an escarpment. The slope is broken here and there by valleys of greater or less size. These are termed *re-entrants* in relation to the higher ground. Tongues of higher ground separate the re-entrants. These are termed *salients* in relation to the lower ground and of course are the same as spurs. It should be noted carefully that the contour system representing a spur is identical with that denoting a re-entrant (see Fig. 27), and beginners are often led into error by this. There are two ways of distinguishing

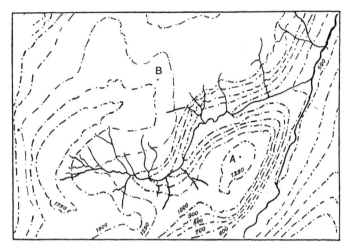

Fig. 24. U-shaped valley. Cwm Glasgwm, Carnarvonshire, a branch of Cwm Penmachno (part of which is seen on the right of the figure). Points to note: parallel trend of the slopes; convex sides; flat bottom; typical corrie or *cirque* found in glacier valleys; steep V-less gradient of tributary streams, which causes such affluent valleys to be termed *hanging*. Contrast this system with the one shown in the previous figure.

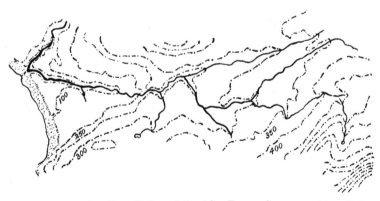

Fig. 25. V-shaped valley. Valley of the Afon Daron, Carnarvonshire. Points to note: the gradual widening out from source to mouth; concave sides; the "nosing" upstream of the contours.

32   POPULAR MAP READING

which of the features is meant. The easier is to look for the streams, remembering that they flow down re-entrants. When there is no stream the contour heights must be appealed to. Fig. 27 shows

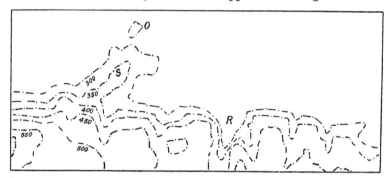

Fig. 26. An escarpment. The contours show an original straight slope broken by erosion. Note the steep slope in one direction; plateau top. A large re-entrant (R) among several others, a spur (S), and an outlier (O) are shown.

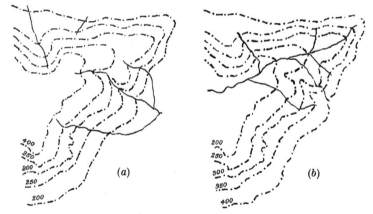

Fig. 27. Identical contour systems showing (a) a salient, (b) a re-entrant.

identical contour systems denoting in the one case a spur and in the other a re-entrant. The only distinction apart from the direction of the streams is that in the former the heights are greater inwards, while in the latter they run higher outwards.

Fig. 28 represents a ridge. The two re-entrants which slope away in opposite directions are characteristic. When the valley-lines are steep and their heads close together, the ridge is a col; when the re-entrants are shallow and their heads comparatively far apart, the ridge is of the saddle variety.

Fig. 28. A ridge. Baroch Fell and Hill Rigg, Cumberland, with connecting ridge shown at X. Note the re-entrants on opposite sides of the ridge.

The section may be summed up by a recapitulation of the rules learnt:

(i) The closer together the contours the steeper the slope, on maps on the same scale.

(ii) A sudden change in the distance apart of contours denotes a sudden change of slope.

(iii) In concave slopes there is a gradual spacing out of contours from top to bottom.

(iv) Streams mark the valley-lines.

(v) Decrease of height towards the centre of a contour system denotes negative relief.

Exercises on Contour Reading

A

(References are to Map II)

1. Mark out the ridge-lines in red and the valley-lines in blue. Choose a small stream and shade its whole basin.
2. Find examples of the following: conical hill, spur, re-entrant, buttress, bluff, gully, col, saddle, ridge, foothill.

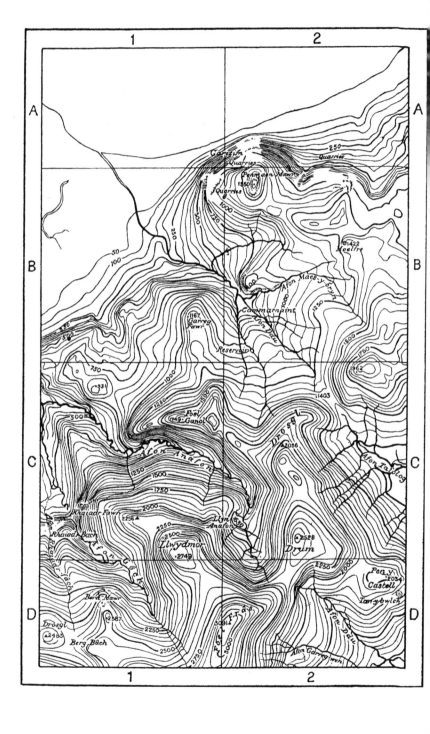

3. Mark the summit and crest-line of Llwydmor, and locate the brow looking north-west.

4. Shade the floor of the valley of the Afon Anafon. Where would you place the dividing line between the upper and the middle course?

5. Mark the points in the valley of the Afon Ddu separating the upper, middle, and lower course.

6. Find examples of convex, concave, and uniform slopes. Which is the commonest, and why?

7. Find examples of: catchment basin, cirque, branch valley, lake, lagoon, meander, pass, outlier, cliff, mudflats.

8. Find a V-shaped valley, a U-shaped valley. Which kind is the more frequent in the district shown? Why?

9. Point out exactly where you would stand on Drosgl Hill (C2) to command a view of the valley of the Afon Tafolog. Explain the reasons for your choice.

10. A main road is shown on the original of Map II. Trace its probable course.

11. By examination of the map, discover the meaning of the word *Afon*. What variant is used in England? Give examples.

12. Discover the meanings of the words *llyn, pen, nant,* and *mawr* which occur on the map, and say to what extent their use is appropriate.

13. Is the valley-line of the Afon Ddu convex or concave? Wholly or in part? Is the same true of the valley of the Afon Anafon?

14. Trace the path you would follow in walking from the summit of Drum to the river confluence at C1—08. Describe the topography of the ground over which you would pass.

B

(N.B. *In the following examples a scale of 1 in. to 1 mile and a vertical interval of 50 ft. should be used*)

1. Draw contours showing three conical hills with (a) a uniform slope, (b) a concave slope, (c) a convex slope.

2. Show by means of contours a hill of irregular shape with two gullies on the west side.

3. Indicate by means of contours an irregular hill indented by a ravine on the east and having a long concave slope towards the west.

4. Show by means of contours two hills joined by a ridge.

5. Draw a contour map of an imaginary island 4 miles by 2, with the ground rising to a hill whose summit is a mile from the eastern shore and is 800 ft. high. All slopes are concave.

6. A ridge projects into the sea as a cape and is continued by a line of three islands. Express this by means of contours, both above and below sea level. Give the islands their appropriate shape and make the undersea contours show the continuation of the land relief.

7. A district has a general slope to the south, but the slope is much broken by re-entrants from which streams issue to join a river flowing at right angles to the slope and at a distance of 2 miles from the foot. Show these facts in a contour map, making all slopes concave.

8. SECTION DRAWING

To get a clear idea of the profile of a feature from a given point of view the best way is to draw a section of the feature. That is, an outline is drawn, and the other parts omitted. The drawing of sections is a useful mechanical exercise and will be frequently used or referred to later in this book. The map reader will do well to make himself proficient in constructing them rapidly. There are several methods of procedure, but we shall begin with the easiest —and most accurate.

Fig. 29 shows the contours representing a hill, of which it is desired to draw a section. First, a decision must be made as to the line of profile required. Then the line is actually drawn (XY in Fig. 29). Parallel with this line another ($X'Y'$ in Fig. 29) is drawn off the map, and a scale constructed on it like the one shown in the figure. Next, vertical lines are dropped from the point of intersection of XY with the various contours to the scale line corresponding in height to the contour which is cut. The profile of the feature is then found by joining up with a smooth curve all the points at which these vertical lines touch the scale lines, as in Fig. 29.

A word must be said about the vertical scale. The horizontal scale of the hill is 1 in. to 1 mile, and on this scale the V.I. of 50 ft. is represented by 1/105 in. nearly. This is the *true vertical scale*. As such a scale would be too small to work with, except under great difficulty, and would show very little relief when the profile was drawn, it is usual to exaggerate the vertical scale to get a convenient length for working purposes and to show up the relief. The amount of exaggeration for the latter purpose varies with the country, but generally speaking in mountainous districts

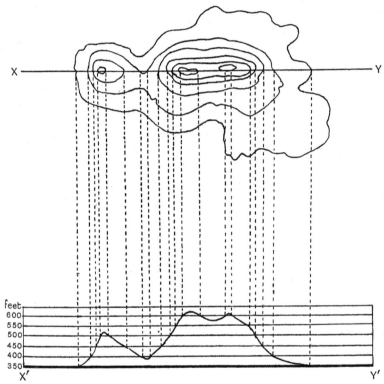

Fig. 29. Section of a hill. Tregonning and Godolphin Hills (146 A 9), Cornwall. The section is longitudinal. It does not give a skyline profile, since the line of section does not coincide with the ridge-line. The difference between the two profiles is seen particularly in the ridge and in the right-hand peak of Tregonning Hill. The vertical scale is exaggerated 10 times (nearly).

the vertical scale should be exaggerated five times (i.e. the V.I. of 50 should be represented by ·05 in. roughly), in hilly districts ten times (V.I. represented by ·1 in. roughly), and in flat country twenty-one times (V.I. represented by ·2 in. nearly). A note should always be added to indicate the exaggeration of the vertical scale.

When the paper on which the section is to be drawn cannot be fixed securely and accurately parallel with the line of section, the foregoing method is difficult. In that case a second method should be adopted. The line along which the section is to be drawn should be decided upon, as before. Then a scale like that in Fig. 29 should be constructed. The distance from X to the point of intersection of XY with the first contour should be measured (with dividers) and the distance laid off along $X'Y'$ on the line corresponding to the contour height. Then the distance from X to the next point of intersection is found and laid off along the next line above on the scale. This is done with each point of intersection in turn, until their places have all been located on the scale. Then the smooth curve is drawn as before, and the section is complete. This is a far quicker method than the first.

It may be noticed that an infinite number of sections may be drawn of the same feature and that thus the profile may be got from all sides. When the line of section runs the length of the feature, the section is *longitudinal*; when it runs across the feature, a *cross-section* is the result.

Exercises on Section Drawing

1. In Fig. 29 draw a straight line at right angles to XY and cutting all the contours twice. Draw a section along this line.

2. Draw longitudinal sections of the three kinds of slope shown in Fig. 17.

3. Draw a longitudinal section of the spur in Fig. 18.

4. In Fig. 24 join AB and draw a section along the line. Then, in Fig. 25, draw a straight line at right angles to the main stream and construct a section along it. What difference is noticed in the profiles of the two valleys?

5. Draw longitudinal sections of the two diagrams given in Fig. 27.

6. Draw sections along and across the ridge at X in Fig. 28.

7. Draw a longitudinal section of the main valley shown in Fig. 22.

8. In Map I join PR and draw a section along the line.

9. In Map III draw a section along the square line 1—2.

10. Turn to your atlas and draw a section through North America along Lat. 40° N.

11. Repeat this exercise, drawing a section through Australia along Lat. 30° S.

9. Reading the Map—First Stage

The reader who has mastered the foregoing pages should now be able to piece together the information given by the map and to form an idea of the topography of a selected area. If he cannot yet read the map in the fullest sense of the word, he should at any rate be able to distinguish the high ground from the low, to trace the general trend of the ridge- and valley-lines, and to recognise the detail of features. Here, however, he is faced with a new problem, if his area is greater than that represented by a square or two of the Popular map, viz. the difficulty of seeing the wood for the trees. The topography of the area must be grasped as a whole, and a comprehensive view is difficult amid a mass of detail. Hence, the reader must learn to reject the irrelevant and unimportant and to seize on main points. The problem is exactly that of the reader of a newspaper, who is faced with producing a short abstract of the leading article after reading it.

Selection of the Main Feature. The best method of procedure is to look for the main lines of high and low ground, i.e. the ridge- and valley-lines, and note the features, not as isolated details, but as parts of a series. When this has been done, the main or dominating feature must be decided upon. It may be a hill commanding the low ground about it; perhaps it is a valley, or a plateau. There can be no hard and fast rule as to its nature. In fact, its dominating character is purely relative, for the main feature of a small area may become an unimportant detail in a wider view.

Relation of Detail to Main Feature. When the main feature has been decided upon, the next step is to fit in with it the details of secondary importance. Thus, the dominant hill may be broken by a ravine on one side and send out a long spur on the other. If the main feature is a valley, it may have important branches, it may widen out or become narrow at certain points, or its sides may be steep and lead up to very high ground. A plateau, on the other hand, may be inclined in some one general direction, be crossed by a line of high ground, or be deeply trenched by a re-entrant. Whatever these secondary details may be, it is important to grasp their relation to the main feature.

Relation of Artificial Features to Topography. The next step is to consider the chief artificial features, i.e. the towns, villages, woods, roads, railways, etc. It is not enough to note their position: their relation to the topography must be understood. The roads will be seen to thread their way between the high ground, ever seeking a compromise between shortness of route and gentleness of slope. The necessity of following level ground is even more imperative for railways. The towns and villages are not sited at hazard, but owe their growth on their particular site to some cause that is as a rule topographical. Some are collecting centres for agricultural or industrial areas. Thus, a big valley is sure to have a town at its mouth or somewhere on the lower course of its river. Others are junction towns or villages, having sprung up at the meeting- or crossing-point of routes, whether water, road, or rail. In our valley, for instance, in addition to its big collecting centre at or near its mouth, there may be a smaller town or village at the junction of some important branch with the main valley.

In other places 'relief' towns occur, usually at the foot of a pass, where travellers rest before attempting the steep grades of the ridge. Other towns have a strategic value and are found in easily defended positions either on high ground commanding the surroundings or at the entrance to a gap or pass.

Purely 'route' towns and villages also occur. These may owe their growth to the break in a route caused by a river and are sited at a bridge or ford. The number of place names compounded with 'bridge' and 'ford' is an indication of the importance of this cause of growth. Other towns lie at the mouth of a river or at the limit of navigation of an estuary.

These factors and their operation are easily understood when applied to towns; but it should be realised that they influence small villages and even isolated farms as well, although other causes are often seen at work in these smaller dwelling sites. Among these may be mentioned the presence of a spring, a stretch of level ground among hills, a good outlook in the case of the country houses of the rich, a sheltered position from the prevailing wind, a southern aspect, etc. Oftener than not, more than one of these causes is at work.

Description of Topography. The map reader is often called upon to describe the topography of an area, and it is part of his equipment to be able to do this. The procedure is the same as that followed in reading the map, and the matter need not be gone over again. It may, however, help in both the reading and the description of topography if an area is chosen and described.

Map III is part of sheet 106 of the O.S. one-inch Popular map and shows a district in the Chilterns. The main feature is the deeply incised gap through the hills which is followed by the Metropolitan and L.N.E.R. route and by the main road from London to Aylesbury. At right angles to the mouth of the gap runs the steep escarpment of the Chilterns, facing north-west, the top of which forms the highest ground in the neighbourhood and dominates the entrance of the pass. The sides of the gap are steep slopes broken by re-entrants, one of which branches out from Great Missenden and is of considerable secondary importance. The slopes are surmounted by small plateaux which fall gradually away to the south-east.

These facts will be grasped more easily if an extract of the more important contours is traced off. Then the gap and the steep face of the escarpment will be prominent, while the Hampden re-entrant and the plateaux on the high ground will stand out clearly as features of secondary importance.

The upper slopes are heavily wooded, except on the edge of the escarpment, which is exposed to the full force of the prevailing south-west wind. The main artificial feature is the road and railway passing through the gap. This route is a natural highway and must have been used from early times. At the mouth of the gap it crosses the old Icknield Way of the Romans, thus giving rise to the junction town of Wendover. The chief factor in the growth of this town, however, is its strategic position as the key of the pass. The village of Great Missenden at the south-east end of the gap and opposite the mouth of the Hampden re-entrant is a junction point of minor roads.

Further Details of Human Interest. The foregoing may be considered sufficient to describe an area of this size, but there are a number of details to which the inexperienced reader's attention may be called. The culminating point of the gap is the spot height 508 on the road, and it has been necessary to make a cutting here for the railway over a distance of more than a mile. The re-entrants and the gap itself are conspicuously streamless. This is due to the porous nature of the rock which does not allow the water to drain off on the surface. The human importance of this is naturally great. The slopes are as a rule too steep and the plateaux too bare of soil and waterless for human habitation, but each re-entrant has its farm or hamlet. The small re-entrants in the eastern slope can contain only one small centre, while the larger valleys on the western side support two or more villages.

A word may be added about place names and their significance. The commonest affix is -den or -dean (O.E. dene = valley), as might well be expected from the nature of the country; but the Celtic combe and -don and the English ridge, bottom, moor, all occur with appropriate reference to local topography. Ham naturally occurs in so English a district, and so does -ton. A number of components refer to some incidental connexion with vegetation (King's Beech, Hunt's Green, Kingsash, Elmhurst, Oakengrove Farm, etc.), birds (Cock's Hill, Swan Bottom, Rook Wood, etc.), and human beings (Potter Row, Prestwood, Durham Farm— i.e. *Deor's ham*, Russell's Farm, etc.). Noticeable too is the prefix 'Little' before Hampden and 'Great' before Missenden. They are due to the Old English custom of planting the overflow population of a village in a subordinate hamlet. Little Hampden is thus the offspring of Great Hampden, which lies a mile to the south-west. Similarly, Great Missenden is no doubt the parent of Little Missenden, a village which is off the map to the south-east.

This is only one of the many marks left by history on the face of the map. The survival of Celtic place names, of evidence of Roman activity, of medieval abbeys and moats in the midst of a setting of typically English rural settlement, recall well-known historical periods. The reader who is satisfied with mere topography and fails to see the human and historical writing on the map misses one of the greatest objects and principal interests of map reading.

Exercises on Map III

1. Give the map references of the highest and lowest land shown on the map and state the height in each case.

2. Draw sections along the lines (*a*) Monument (A1) to the ½ in Baddington (A2); (*b*) square-line 1—2 from the road junction south-east of Bottom Farm to the extreme north of the map; (*c*) the main road from point 434 in Great Missenden to point 431 in Wendover.

3. Describe the country shown in square B3.

4. Write a geographical description of a walk from Wendover through the Hale, Halton Wood, and Haddington Hill.

5. Enlarge the area shown in square A2 so as to make the scale four times as big as it is in the O.S. map. Show contours for every 100 ft. What is the scale of your drawing?

6. Trace the 800-foot contour on Coombe Hill on to a piece of paper and measure the area of the ground within it. To what topographical type does it belong?

7. Find examples of convex and concave slopes, bluff, buttress.

8. Trace the contours showing the re-entrant running north from Hampden Bottom, and mark on your tracing the valley-line, the foot of the slopes, and the head of the valley.

9. What is the difference in height between (a) the summit of Coombe Hill and Wendover Station; (b) Kingsash (B3) and Durham Farm (B3); (c) the Camp on Bacombe Hill and Wellwick Farm (A2); and (d) Dunsmore and Hampden Bottom (C2)?

10. State roughly the course of the ridge-lines and describe the drainage system of the area.

11. Consult a geological map and describe the reasons for the absence of streams.

12. Say how you consider the valley traced in Question 8 was formed.

13. Explain the position of Durham Farm, Little Hampden, Dunsmore, Honorend Farm, the Hale, Great Missenden, Bottom Farm.

14. Consult a good dictionary and discover the original meanings of the components *ham*, *ton*, *dene*, and *don*. Find places whose names are compounded with them and discuss their appropriateness in each case.

15. What archeological remains appear on the map? Which of them are Roman?

16. What characteristics do most of the archeological remains have in common? What connexion have these with local topography?

17. Discuss the positions of the ancient camps shown in the area.

18. Describe as far as you can from the map the occupations of the inhabitants of the area, and discuss the density of population.

19. What evidence can you gather from the map of Roman, Old English, and medieval history?

20. Find the Wendover gap in an atlas map of England and discuss its importance. Mention any other gaps that occur through the Chilterns.

Revision Exercises, I

1. State what information is given in (a) the margin, (b) the frame, of an O.S. one-inch Popular map.

2. Describe with the help of a diagram the uses of map squares. How may more exact references be given?

3. Turn to Map III and give the map references of Lee, King's Wood, Lanes End, Bacombe Warren, Dutchlands Farm.

4. Explain simply what is meant by a bearing. Find the bearings (on Map III) from point 433 in Wendover to the Monument on Coombe Hill (A1), the Hale (A3), point 508 on the Wendover-Great Missenden road, and point 360 on the Wendover-Aylesbury road.

5. If you start from point 668 (B2) and walk directly on a bearing

of 39° for 3 miles and 1 furlong, at what point named on the map will you then be?

6. How far is it from point 431 in Wendover to point 434 in Great Missenden (*a*) 'as the crow flies', (*b*) by road? Which is the shorter? By how many yards?

7. Measure the distance by road and 'as the crow flies' from point 433 in Wendover to point 731 at St Leonards (A3). Say how much shorter the direct route is in yards.

8. Find and write down the map references of: a park, a trigonometrical point, a bridge under, and a bridge over the railway, a church with tower, a church without tower or spire, a village with post- and telegraph-office, a spot height, a footpath, and an inn.

9. Pick out five names in Map III which are printed in different type and explain the uses of each kind of type.

10. Name and give the map references of six objects which are shown on Map III larger than they really are.

11. What is the minimum width of a main road? How wide should it be shown if drawn to scale? Why is it drawn wider on the map?

12. Calculate the area of Cockshoots Wood (B2).

13. Name the end points of (*a*) two minor roads, (*b*) two narrow roads, (*c*) two footpaths.

14. What is the shortest route by road from Chivery Inn (A3) to Smalldean Farm (B2)?

15. What route would you follow (*a*) on foot, (*b*) by car, from Great Missenden to Kingswood Inn (B3)?

16. Draw or trace a sketch map showing how much of the area shown in Map III would be left above water if the sea rose 700 ft. Insert an undersea contour for 25 fathoms. Colour or shade your map to show up the facts.

17. Draw contour systems representing (*a*) a conical hill with uniform slopes, (*b*) an escarpment with three spurs and two re-entrants, giving the middle spur a convex end-slope and the two outer ones concave end-slopes.

18. You have a fragment of an O.S. one-inch Popular map on which no contour heights are shown, but only two spot heights, 331 and 639, occur. How could you deduce (*a*) which way the slopes ran, and (*b*) the heights of the contours?

19. Draw the contours of a U-shaped valley. After consulting a book on Physical Geography, describe how such a valley is formed.

20. After consulting a Physical Geography text-book, describe the formation of an alluvial fan, a mortlake, a flood plain, a gorge, and a glacier lake. Illustrate your answer with diagrams of the features.

21. Say what topographical causes influence the growth of towns. Give examples, if possible.

22. What features influence the choice of site in the case of small villages and isolated dwellings?

23. What topographical names of Celtic origin do you know of? Explain their meaning and discuss their historical significance.

24. In what way does man influence local topography? Base your answer on the area shown in Map III.

25. How does local topography influence man's (*a*) occupations, (*b*) choice of dwelling site?

CHAPTER III

THE PROBLEM OF THE SLOPE

10. Gradients

So far slopes have been characterised as steep or gentle, the terms 'steep' and 'gentle' being used in their ordinary vague sense. But a number of problems in engineering, transport, and military operations depend for their solution on the exact measurement of

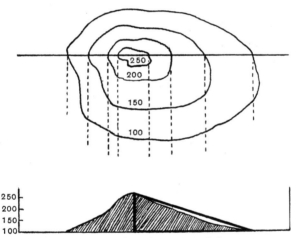

Fig. 30. The triangular nature of slopes.

the degree of steepness of slopes, and apart from this necessity it is desirable that map readers should be able to form their ideas with an accurate and definite knowledge of the facts. To do this requires a little calculation based on the information afforded by the contours of the map.

Any given slope may be regarded as forming a right-angled

triangle, the bounding lines being formed by an imaginary base which is assumed to be horizontal, the vertical interval which is perpendicular to the base, and the slope of the ground which is the hypotenuse. The last is seldom or never a straight line in actual fact, but may be represented by a straight line showing the general mean slope. The section of the slope of a hill illustrates this clearly (see Fig. 30).

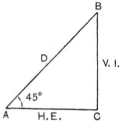

Fig. 31 a. V.I. = H.E.

Any given slope, therefore, may be represented by a triangle *ABC* (see Fig. 31 *a*) in which the hypotenuse *AB* stands for the slope of the ground and is known as the *distance* (**D.** for short).

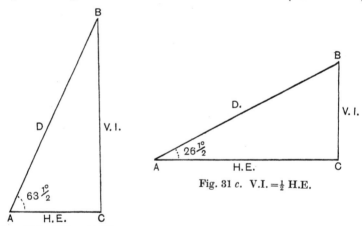

Fig. 31 b. V.I. = 2 H.E.

Fig. 31 c. V.I. = ½ H.E.

AC represents the plan of *AB* and is termed the *horizontal equivalent* (H.E.). The perpendicular *BC* is of course the vertical interval (V.I.). The angle *BAC* is the *angle of slope*. Measurements on the map give the H.E., and the V.I. is found by means of the contours.

It is evident that the angle of slope depends on the ratio of V.I. to H.E. For instance, in Fig. 31 *a* where the V.I. = H.E., the angle of slope is 45°. If the V.I. is doubled the angle of slope is increased to 63½°, as in Fig. 31 *b*. If the H.E. is doubled, as in Fig. 31 *c*, the angle of slope is reduced to 26½°.

The same results may be obtained by halving the H.E. in the first case and halving the V.I. in the second.

Hence, the degree of slope is often expressed by the ratio V.I. : H.E. or the fraction $\frac{V.I.}{H.E.}$. It is usual to reduce the fraction so as to make the numerator unity. The result is then termed the gradient of the slope.[1]

For example, if the distance between two places as measured on the map (i.e. the H.E.) is found to be 300 yds. (or 900 ft.), and the difference in height to be 100 ft. (V.I.), then the gradient is $\frac{100}{900} = \frac{1}{9}$. In speaking of the gradient, this ratio is read as 'one in nine', and means that for every foot of ascent a distance of 9 ft. is travelled horizontally.

Exercises on Gradients, I

1. If the V.I. is 50 ft., find the gradients of the following slopes whose lengths on the map are found to be respectively 200, 400, 450, 5000, 6500, 750, 1750, 2750 yds.

2. Find the gradients of the slopes between places with:

(*a*) a difference in height of 180 ft.; a distance apart of 1620 yds.;
(*b*)   ,,   ,,   210 ft.;   ,,   2520 yds.;
(*c*)   ,,   ,,   72 ft.;   ,,   216 yds.;
(*d*)   ,,   ,,   59 ft.;   ,,   1416 yds.;
(*e*)   ,,   ,,   138 ft.;   ,,   2967 yds.

3. On the accompanying diagram find the gradient of the slopes:

from *B* to *A*, *C*, and *D*;
from *E* to *F* and from *F* to *G*;
from *H* to *I* and *J*;
from *B* to *K* and *L*.

---

[1] In practical engineering and in much mathematical work the gradient is calculated from the ratio V.I. : D. The difference is negligible in gentle slopes.

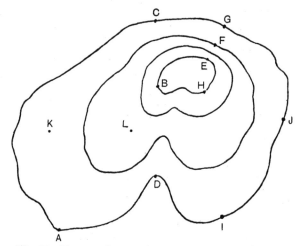

Fig. 32. For exercises on the measurement of gradients.

Conversion of Gradient into Angle of Slope and vice versa

Instead of expressing the degree of slope by the gradient, the angular measurement may be given. Thus, the steepness of a certain slope may be described either by its gradient of 1/20 or by its angle of slope of 3°. The map reader is often faced with the problem of converting one method of description into the other.

To find the Angle of Slope from the Gradient. There are three ways of doing this:

(*a*) Construct a triangle to scale and measure the angle with a protractor.

(*b*) The fraction $\frac{\text{V.I.}}{\text{H.E.}}$ is known in trigonometry as the tangent of the angle subtended by the V.I. Reduce the fraction to a decimal and look up the corresponding angle in a book of tables.

(*c*) A rough-and-ready method is to multiply the gradient by 60. The results obtained are only approximate. They are useless for gradients of over $\frac{1}{6}$.

To find the Gradient from the Angle of Slope. This is more difficult, but is less frequently required. It may be done in any one of the following ways:

(a) Divide the angle of slope by 60. Thus, an angle of slope of 3° gives a gradient of $\frac{3}{60} = \frac{1}{20}$. As before, this method is only approximate. It is useless for angles of more than 10°.

(b) If the length of one side is known, a triangle may be constructed to scale and the gradient found from it.

(c) Read off the value of the tangent of the angle from trigonometrical tables and express the value in the form usual for gradients.

Exercises on Gradients, II

1. The gradient of a certain hill is 1 in 8; what is the angle of slope?
2. The gradient of another hill is 1 in 120; find the angle of slope.
3. If the angle of slope of a hill is 10°, find the gradient.
4. What is the gradient corresponding to an angle of slope of 1°? of 4°?
5. Measured on the map (scale 1 in. to 1 mile), the distance from A to B is 2 in. The difference in height is 440 ft. What is the gradient? the angle of slope?
6. A is $1\frac{1}{2}$ in. from B on the map (scale 1 in. to 1 mile). The height of A is 302 ft. above sea level, and that of B is 500 ft. Find the gradient and the angle of slope of a straight line drawn from A to B.

Standard Slopes. The following table gives some idea of the value of certain slopes. But to appreciate the real meaning of the stan-

Angle of slope	Gradient	Description	Remarks
Less than 1°	1/60	Gentle	Steep railway gradient
1° to 3°	1/60 to 1/20	Moderate	Cyclists walk
3° to 6°	1/20 to 1/10	Stiff	Horse-drawn vehicles proceed at a walk
6° to 12°	1/10 to 1/5	Steep	Cars find gradient difficult and change gear
12° to 20°	1/5 to 1/3	Very steep	Horses descend obliquely on slopes of over 15°, and horse-drawn vehicles cannot ascend. The 'stunt' limit for cars is 1/2·5
20° to 30°	1/3 to 1/2		
Over 30°	1/2	Precipitous	Can only be climbed by men using their hands

dards one should find local hills with slopes approximately equal to those on the table and familiarise oneself with the significance of 3° of slope, a gradient of 1 in 5, etc., by walking, cycling, and riding up and down them.

Scale of Standard Slopes. It is obviously inconvenient to be constantly making large numbers of calculations in order to discover the degree of steepness of the various slopes along a certain road or in the approaches to some hill. The difficulty can be avoided by the construction of a scale of standard slopes.

The principle of construction may be explained simply with the aid of a little drawing. As the scale of 1 in. = 1 mile is too small for convenience, the scale of 25 in. = 1 mile will be used. Draw a straight line of convenient length, say 6 in., to serve as the H.E. On the scale selected the V.I. of 50 ft. is represented by ·24 in. $\left(\frac{25 \times 50}{5280} = \frac{125}{528} = ·24\right)$. Draw another straight line parallel to the H.E. and at a distance of ·24 in. from it. From a point X at one end of the H.E. draw straight lines making the angles 3°, 6°, 12°, 20°, 30° respectively with the H.E. and cutting the second line. Drop perpendiculars from the points of intersection to the H.E. Then measure the distance from X along the H.E. to the foot of each perpendicular. The results obtained are the H.E.'s corresponding to the respective degrees of slope. See Fig. 33.

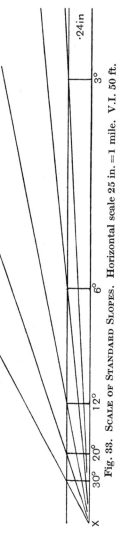

Fig. 33. SCALE OF STANDARD SLOPES. Horizontal scale 25 in. = 1 mile. V.I. 50 ft.

But mechanical difficulties prevent this method from being used with most scales. Hence, the following method is suggested: In the triangle *ABC* (Fig. 34), let *AC* represent the H.E. and *BC* the V.I. of 50 ft. Let the angle of slope *BAC* be 20°. As shown in the table on page 51, the ratio of V.I. to H.E., when the angle of slope is 20°, is 1 : 3. That is, if the V.I. = 50 ft., the H.E. = 50 ft. ×

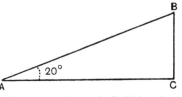

Fig. 34. As the angle *BAC* is 20°, *BC* = ⅓*AC*.

3 = 150 ft. or 50 yds. If the value is worked out for each angle in the table, the results will be found to be as follows:

For a V.I. of 50 ft.

angle of 1° gives H.E. of 1000 yds. or ·568 mile.
,,   3°   ,,   333   ,,   ·189 ,,
,,   6°   ,,   167   ,,   ·095 ,,
,,   12°   ,,   83   ,,   ·047 ,,
,,   20°   ,,   50   ,,   ·028 ,,
,,   30°   ,,   33   ,,   ·019 ,,

A scale may be constructed by one of two methods:

Method 1. Draw a straight line of convenient length (say 4 in.). Find on the protractor the scale of yards. Set the compasses to the several distances required and mark them off on the line. The scale of gradients is then complete.

Method 2. Draw a straight line as before. Set the compasses to the mile distances given above and mark them off on the line. The scale is then complete and should be the same as if constructed by method 1. See Fig. 35.

Having constructed the scale of standard slopes, the gradients

Fig. 35. A gradient scale for use with the O.S. Popular 1-in. map. The vertical lines are contours. On their distance apart depends the degree of slope, as shown by the scale.

of an area under study may be tested and a fairly accurate idea obtained of the degree of slope. After some practice the scale may be dispensed with, as the reader will then have become familiar with judging the slopes by the length of the H.E. It should be remembered that, if a scale of gradients is drawn for use with, say, one-inch maps, a new scale must be drawn when the reader changes to, say, a six-inch map.

Exercises on Gradients, III

(*The map references are to* Map III)

1. What is the gradient of the slope from Great Missenden Abbey to the **p** of Camp? Calculate approximately the angle of slope.

2. Find the gradient of the slope from Wendover Station to the camp on Bacombe Hill. What is the approximate angle of slope?

3. Measure the distance from point 434 in Great Missenden to point 508 just east of Smalldean Farm and find the mean gradient of the road between these points.

4. Find the shortest distance by road from Wendover Church to the Hale. What is the gradient of the steepest part? What is the mean gradient?

5. A cyclist goes by road from Little London (B2) to Kingsash. Where does he freewheel? Must he walk any part of the way? If so, where?

(N.B. *Use the scale of gradients whenever possible in the following questions*)

6. Find slopes which may be characterised as 'gentle', 'moderate', 'stiff', 'steep'.

7. You wish to go by car from Great Missenden to Lee. Say what route you select, giving reasons. What part, if any, of your way would lie downhill?

8. Find a gradient which no car could ascend. What do you notice about the paths which go up the slope?

9. When the farmer drives his gig from Durham Farm to Lee, is there any part of his route at which he must walk his horse? If so, where?

10. What is the easiest gradient by any route marked on the map from Rignall (C2) to Dunsmore?

11. Account for the bend in the road by the Water Works.

12. Measure the shortest possible cross-country route from Wendover Church to the summit of Baddington Hill. Remembering what you have read about gradients, do you think your map measurement gives the real distance?

13. Calculate the difference between the map measurement required by the previous question and the real distance along the ground.

14. A motorist is driving from Wendover to Scrubs (B2) via Dunsmore. Will he probably change to a lower gear on the way? If so, at what point? If he returns by the same route, will a change of gear be necessary anywhere?

Exercises on Gradients, IV

(N.B. *In all the following exercises, except where otherwise stated, the scale used should be* 1/63,360 *and the V.I.* 50 *ft.*)

1. Draw an imaginary hill with all its gradients between 1/20 and 1/12. The lowest contour should be 300 ft., the highest 500 ft.

2. Draw an imaginary island 5 miles long and 3 broad, with the long axis running east and west. A conical hill whose summit is 1000 ft. high and 1 mile from the west coast, slopes steeply to the west with a convex face, but descends in a concave slope to the east, ending in a gentle slope for the last 2 miles.

3. Draw a map of an imaginary island with two hills, one 400 ft., the other 200 ft. high. Slopes below 200 ft. are gentle; those above 200 ft. are stiff. The island is 6 miles by 4. Insert a river, and a road across the island.

4. A valley 3 miles long lies between the spurs of a hill. Several branch valleys re-enter the spurs on either side. The summit of the hill is 600 ft. high. A stream flows down the valley, descending less than 50 ft. in the last 1½ miles. Express these facts in a map, making the 100-foot contour the lowest shown.

5. A flat-topped hill is connected by a ridge with a conical hill to the north. Their distance apart from summit to summit is 4 miles. The flat-topped hill is 800 ft. high, the conical hill 1000 ft. The conical hill has stiff uniform slopes on all sides, except towards the ridge, where the slope is concave and soon becomes gentle. The slope of the flat-topped hill is convex to the south, but is everywhere gentle. Express this in a map. The 100-foot contour is the lowest to be shown.

6. A valley running from north to south ends in a bay 4 miles wide. The valley is closed on the north by a ridge connecting two conical hills, from which projecting spurs form promontories enclosing the bay. The distance from the top of the ridge to the shore of the bay

is 6 miles. Each of the hills is 1500 ft. high, but the eastern spur is lower than the western, descending in a gentle slope to the valley floor, while the western spur descends in a stiff, concave slope. A river flows down the valley from the ridge with a descent of 50 ft. in the last 3 miles. Express these facts in a sketch map.

7. On the map drawn for the previous question, show a village with a church with spire, a post- and telegraph-office, and an inn. Trace the path of roads running out of the valley east and west, neither of which has a gradient of more than 1/20. Insert a bridge and a lighthouse.

11. ROAD SECTIONS

The accurate measurement of gradients not only satisfies the natural craving for definite and exact knowledge which forms part of the character of even the least inquisitive of human beings, but it also enables the map reader to realise the effect of different degrees of slope on human activity. One of the commonest problems arising out of the slope of the ground is that which faces the motorist, cyclist, or other road passenger in attempting a new route. Will he have any steep gradients to climb? If so, will the car be able to reach the top? How much of the way will the cyclist be forced to walk?

These and many similar questions are best answered by a simple device for showing graphically the gradients of a given route. It consists of a section drawn so as to show the ups and downs along the route and is so helpful that published road guides are as a rule not complete without them.[1] But they are easily drawn in a few minutes and are almost indispensable in a close study of an intended route.

There is no difference in principle between the drawing of road sections and other sections. In fact, if the road is straight, the procedure is the same. When the road is curved, as of course it usually is, the distance from contour to contour must be measured on the map and laid off on a straight line. When the points at

[1] Gall and Inglis's *Contour Road Book of Great Britain* gives sections for all the main roads in the kingdom.

which contours intersect the road have all been plotted on this line, perpendiculars are erected at each point equal to the respective heights of the contours on the selected scale. The tops of the perpendiculars are then joined by a smooth curve, which represents the section of the road. Thus, in Fig. 36, if A is the starting-point and B the point at which the first contour cuts the road, the distance from A to B is measured and its length $A'B'$ laid off on the straight line $A'D'$. The distance BC is then measured and laid off as $B'C'$ along $A'D'$. The same procedure is followed with all the other inter-contour portions of the road till the end is reached at D.

Let the selected vertical scale be ·1 in. to 100 ft. Then the next step is to erect at B', C', etc., perpendiculars equal to their respective contour heights according to scale. $B'B''$ is thus ·4 in., $C'C''$ ·4 in., and so on. The curve $A''B''C''D''$ is then drawn and is the required section.

To finish off the section and increase its practical utility on the road, insert the names of places of interest and the steeper slopes together with the gradients or angles of slope. Fig. 37 shows a section of the road over the Pennines from Kirkoswald through Alston to Wear Head. This road has the interest of ascending at Pennine Ridge to a greater height than any other road in England. The vertical scale has been exaggerated, as usual, in order to show up the slopes.

Exercises on Road Sections

(References are to Map III)

1. Draw a section of the road from Great Missenden to Wendover, using a vertical scale of ·2 in. = 50 ft. Try to draw another section of the same road, using the natural vertical scale (i.e. without exaggeration) of ·002 in. = 50 ft. What practical difficulty is encountered?

2. Draw a section of the road which leaves the main route near the 34th mile (B2) through Kingsash as far·as the cross-road at Swan Bottom. Insert the names of two villages along the way and mark the position and steepness of the sharpest gradient.

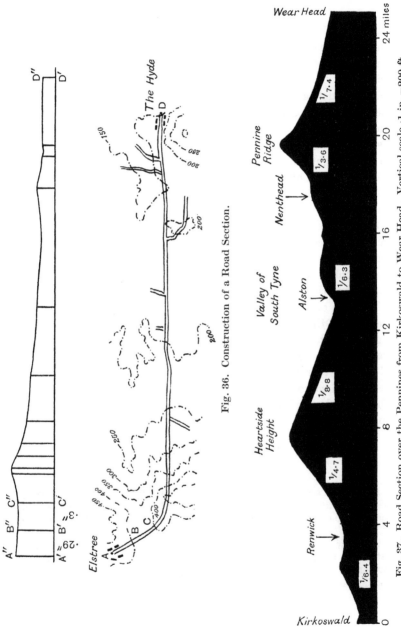

Fig. 36. Construction of a Road Section.

Fig. 37. Road Section over the Pennines from Kirkoswald to Wear Head. Vertical scale ·1 in. =200 ft.
Horizontal scale 1 in ≡ 4 miles.

3. Draw a section of the railway, allowing for the cutting. What are the two gradients?

4. Draw a road section of the route from Great Missenden via Potter Row to the Water Works (A3).

5. If you were about to draw the section of a road in a hilly district like the Highlands of Scotland, would it be necessary to exaggerate the vertical scale? Satisfy yourself that your answer is correct by drawing a road section from a map of the Highlands.

12. INTERVISIBILITY OF POINTS AND DEAD GROUND

Everyone knows that to obtain a good view an elevated point should be reached. The reason for this is that when the viewpoint is relatively low, small objects, like trees and minor topographical features, are apt to intercept much of the view; whereas from an

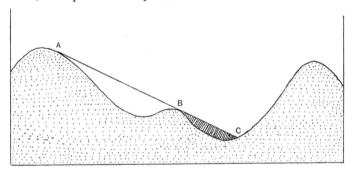

Fig. 38. The stippled area is the section of a hill. *ABC* is a line of sight from *A*. As the line grazes an obstacle at *B*, all the space shaded between *B* and *C* is shut out from view. The ground thus hidden is *dead*.

elevated point one overlooks them. When the view is interrupted by an object or feature, an area of greater or less extent is hidden from sight. This area is known as *dead ground* and is of great importance, especially in military operations. A visit to the viewpoint shows the observer the exact extent of his view. But such a visit is not always possible, and a knowledge of the view to be obtained and of the position of dead ground may be acquired from an examination of the map.

In some cases the matter is obvious. It has already been seen that on regular concave slopes there is a clear view from top to bottom, while on convex slopes the view is interrupted. But when the ground is broken and various features or underfeatures stand up here and there, it is not always easy to say whether they can be overlooked. The first step to take is to recognise these possible obstacles; then one will be able to calculate whether and to what extent they interrupt the view.

Intervisibility of Points. The simplest form of problem involved is to discover whether a certain objective can be seen from a given viewpoint. The map should be examined and possible obstacles noted. If the intervening ground is concave and no possible obstacles exist, the points are intervisible. If a possible obstacle exists, then its effect should be calculated by the method which will now be explained. Either the viewpoint and the objective are of equal height or they are not.

(i) *Intervisibility of Points of Equal Height.* In the first case the matter is simple. For, obviously, to interrupt the view the obstacle must be as high as the viewpoint and the objective.[1]

(ii) *Intervisibility of Points of Different Height.* If the viewpoint is higher than the objective, then the possible obstacle will only intercept the view if it stands above the line of sight, i.e. the straight line joining the viewpoint to the objective. Thus, suppose A and B in Fig. 39 are two posts 4 ft. and 2 ft. high respectively standing on level ground at a distance of 12 ft. apart. Let the top of A be the viewpoint and the top of B the objective. Then VO is the line of sight. Now, if two other posts, C and D, each 3 ft. high, are placed in line with A and B, so that C is 2 ft. from A and D 2 ft. from B, it is clear that D projects above the line of sight and

---

[1] The curvature of the Earth must sometimes be considered. It amounts to 8 in. × the square of the distance in miles, i.e. 8 in. for the first mile (8 in. × 1^2 = 8 in.), 32 in. for the second (8 in. × 2^2 = 32 in.), 72 in. for the third (8 in. × 3^2 = 72 in.), and so on. For short distances the curvature may be ignored, since a margin should always be allowed for possible bushes, etc., on the obstacle. But for distances over 8 miles it should be taken into account.

intercepts the view, while C does not, though both C and D are of the same height. This is because the gradient of the line of sight is steeper than that of $C'O$, but less steep than that of $D'O$. (The

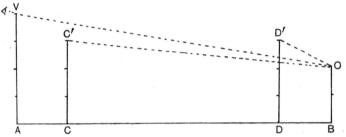

Fig. 39. INTERVISIBILITY OF POINTS. V is the viewpoint, O the objective. As the gradient of $C'O$ is less than that of the line of sight, the obstacle $C'C$ does not obstruct the view.

gradient of VO is $\frac{2}{12} = \frac{1}{6}$; that of $C'O$, $\frac{1}{10}$; that of $D'O$, $\frac{1}{2}$.) Hence, all the map reader has to do to decide whether the view is interrupted or not is to find the gradient of the line of sight by taking the

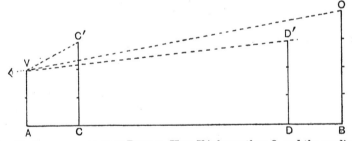

Fig. 40. INTERVISIBILITY OF POINTS. Here V is lower than O, and the gradient must be reckoned back from C', O, and D' to V. As the gradient of $C'V$ is greater than that of OV, the obstacle $C'C$ obstructs the view; while $D'D$ does not obstruct it, because the gradient of $D'V$ is less than that of OV.

difference in height of the viewpoint and the objective as numerator and the distance between the points as denominator. Then he must find the gradient of the line from the top of the possible obstacle to the objective in the same way. If the gradient of the line of sight is the steeper, the view is not interrupted; if it is less steep, the obstacle shuts off the view.

If the viewpoint is lower than the objective, the calculation is made in the same way; only, the gradients are measured from the objective to the viewpoint (see **Fig. 40**).

Graphical Methods. Two graphical methods may be used to illustrate the intervisibility of points or even to discover whether points are intervisible:

(i) Using squared paper let distance be measured along the horizontal axis on a convenient scale and height along the vertical axis. Plot the position of the viewpoint and the objective and join them by a straight line. Next, plot the position of intervening objects. If these are on or above the line joining viewpoint and objective, they intercept the line of sight; if they are below the line, they do not intercept the line of sight.

(ii) Draw a section along the straight line joining the viewpoint and the objective, and it will be evident whether the view is intercepted or not.

Dead Ground. To find what area is dead ground from a given viewpoint requires a longer, though scarcely more difficult, calculation. It is seldom necessary to locate the dead ground in every direction; usually, only that which lies within a given sector is required. The first step is to look for irregularities and positive relief within the sector. If any are found, they must be dealt with one by one, and it is best to begin with those nearest the viewpoint, since the others may lie in dead ground and the time spent on them will therefore be wasted. Examine the obstacle and note whether the gradient of its far slope is steeper than that of the line of sight from the viewpoint to the top of the obstacle. If it is steeper, there will be dead ground; otherwise, there will be none (see **Fig. 42**). This may usually be seen at a glance. If there is dead ground, use a graphical method to show where the line of sight comes to the ground beyond the obstacle and to find the side limits

Graphical Method 1.
(Horizontal scale 1 in. = 1 mile.)

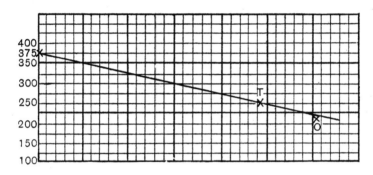

Graphical Method 2.

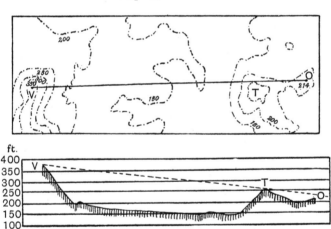

Method of Calculation.

Between V and O there is only one feature higher than either, viz. the hill T.
Therefore this hill is the only possible obstacle.

Distance from V to O = 3 miles = 5280 × 3 ft.
Difference in height   = 181 ft.
Therefore gradient of line of sight = 181/5280 × 3 = 1/88·06.
Distance from T to O = ·58 miles = 5280 × ·58 ft.
Difference in height   = 36 ft.
Therefore gradient   = 36/5280 × ·58 = 1/85·1.
Hence, O is not visible from V.

Fig. **41.** Methods of finding whether given points are intervisible or not, illustrated and compared.

of the dead ground. The latter is usually at the lowest contour of the
obstacle; if it is not, it must be found by trial. These three points
on the margin of the dead ground are sufficient to enable the dead
ground to be sketched in, if the obstacle is small and has a regular
profile. If there are irregularities, other limits should be found by
discovering where a line of sight meets the ground after passing
over the irregularities. Then join up the limits with a smooth curve.
The result will be an elongated shadow of the obstacle, which is
the dead ground. Shade the area.

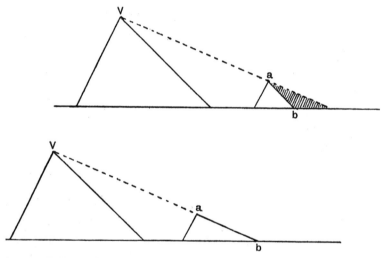

Fig. 42. Effect of further slopes on intervisibility. The conditions are identical
in the figures, except that in the first the further slope *ab* has a greater gradient
than the line of sight. In that figure therefore dead ground occurs. But not in
the second, where the gradient of *ab* is not greater than that of the line of sight.

A cross-section of the obstacle at right angles to the line of
sight over the highest point of the obstacle will often be found
useful in difficult cases (i) for determining the side limits, and
(ii) for giving some idea of irregularities and of the shape of the
shadow.

In actual practice, it is often difficult to find the exact height of ground: small areas of high ground are not always marked with spot heights. Moreover, bushes, trees, etc., not shown on the map may increase the height of the obstacle. Hence, it is best to allow a margin of some feet even when the exact height of the obstacle itself is known. If there is a wood at the top of the obstacle, some

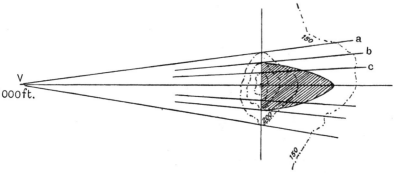

Fig. 43. Method of plotting an area of dead ground. Sections along the rays *a*, *b*, *c*, etc., show where the line of sight reaches the ground. These points are plotted and joined by a smooth curve, the area within which is then shaded.

30 or 40 ft. should be allowed.[1] It should be remembered, therefore, that the results obtained from the calculations described are only approximate. But the calculations are not useless, since many cases occur in which, after the greatest reasonable margin has been allowed, the points in question are found to be intervisible; while in many others the line of sight is with equal certainty intercepted. There remain the borderline cases about which there is no certainty. It is something at any rate to be able to discover this.

[1] The curvature of the Earth and refraction also affect the question; but the calculations they involve require far too much time for practical use in the field.

Exercises on Intervisibility of Points and Dead Ground

(N.B. *References are to* Map IV)

1. Find by inspection whether the following points are visible from *B*: *T*, *G*, *P*, *A*. Use graphical method 1 to prove your answer.

2. Find by inspection whether the following points are visible from *H*: *D*, *C*, *R*, *T*. Use graphical method 2 to prove your answer.

3. Are *B* and *H* intervisible? Prove your answer by method 2.

4. What possible interruptions are there of the line of sight from *H* to *O*? Calculate whether the points are intervisible.

5. In a view from *B* to *Q*, what possible obstacles are there to the line of sight? Calculate whether *B* and *Q* are intervisible.

6. After inspection say whether *K* is visible from *H*. Write out a full calculation to show whether your answer is correct.

7. Find whether *D* and *G* are intervisible.

8. Which of the points *P*, *B*, and *G* are visible to a scout at *C*?

9. Are *P* and *R* intervisible? Prove your answer by a graphical method.

10. Does the hillock at *T* come into a view seen from *R*?

11. Would a building at *D* come into a photograph taken from *T* looking south-east?

12. What ground is likely to interrupt the view from *P* to *T*? Can *T* be seen?

13. What ground within a sector of 20° would be dead to a spectator at *N* looking towards *O*?

14. What ground in the sector *HD*, *HE* (produced to the edge of the map) would be dead to an observer at *H*?

15. Is *E* visible from *A*? And how much of the re-entrant *F* is dead ground from *A*?

16. What ground in the direction of *F* would be dead to an observer at *D*? Include a sector of 10° and shade the dead ground on the map.

17. A mast at *H* is just visible from *P*. What is the height of the mast?

18. *D* is not visible from *A*. How high a tower must be erected at *A* to obtain a view of *D*?

19. An observer at *G* cannot see *K*. How high must he ascend in a balloon to obtain a view of *K*? And how high must an observer at *K* ascend in order to see *G*?

20. An aeroplane flying over the point *B* can just see *K*. At what height was the aeroplane flying above *B*?

13. Construction of View from a Given Point

We now come to one of the chief objectives of our subject, and it may be as well to glance back at the ground covered so as to be able to grasp the methods of our approach. After making acquaintance with the map and its symbols, we dealt with the significance of contour systems and endeavoured to make these combinations of lines call up to our mind the profiles of the features represented. We even tried to combine these features into a comprehensive view of a whole area. This was the first of our objectives. But something was missing, and our view was vague and ill-defined. That defect has been removed by a study of gradients, by practice in deciding whether individual points are visible from a given place, and by exercises in determining areas of dead ground from a chosen viewpoint. We should now therefore be able to achieve the second great object in map reading, viz. the power of visualising the topographical scene from a selected standpoint.

To call up the scene thus by a glance at the map is no easy matter, but skill in doing so is rapidly acquired by practice. The first aim should be to trace the path of the skyline. The only sure way of learning to do this is to begin with a mechanical method which will gradually train the eye to pick out the bounding lines of the horizon.

Method of Constructing the Skyline. First choose a viewpoint and decide what sector of the horizon the view is to include. From the viewpoint draw straight lines to form the limits of the chosen sector. Draw other straight lines from the viewpoint to cut prominent features, both negative and positive, within the sector (see Fig. 44). Then draw sections along all these rays. In each section join the viewpoint by a straight line with the highest point within sight. Then the point at which this line touches the ground is on the skyline.

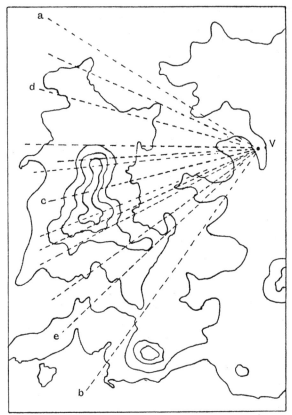

Fig. 44. Construction of Skyline, Stage 1. Open divided scale of yards
for use with a one-inch map.

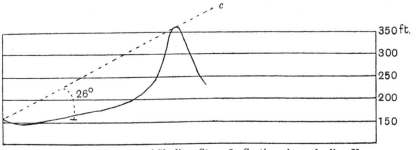

Fig. 45. Construction of Skyline, Stage 2. Section along the line Vc,
with ray and angle measurement.

Next measure the angle subtended by the greatest height within view in each section (see Fig. 45). On a separate paper draw a straight line to represent the horizontal plane of the viewpoint. Choose a vertical scale to represent the degrees measured in the sections. Plot each point in the skyline according to this scale and to a suitable horizontal scale. Join the points plotted thus by a regular curve, which then represents the skyline (see Fig. 46). The procedure is much the same as in section drawing, and the more points plotted the greater the accuracy of the result.

Exercises on the Construction of the Skyline

1. Construct the skyline as seen from point 607 (Map III, C3) within a sector bounded on the east by a straight line from the viewpoint through point 639 (B3) and on the west by a ray through point 815 (B1).

2. Construct the skyline in a view from Russell's Farm (Map III, B2) bounded by rays through the summit of Baddington Hill and through point 626 at Hunts Green (B3).

Note. Other exercises should be chosen on local maps. The sector of view should not be too great, especially in broken country, or else the exercise becomes long and tedious.

When the reader has done two or three of these exercises, he should be able to form a pretty good idea of the path of the skyline on a map. It should be observed that the line is not continuous like a ridge-line, but is apt to stop short suddenly, to continue on a nearer or more distant line on high ground (see Fig. 47). Furthermore, the skyline path does not necessarily follow the ridge-lines: it sometimes cuts them at right angles.

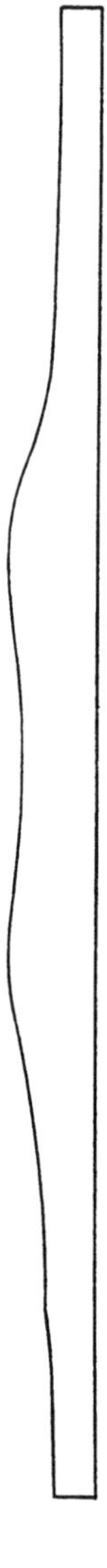

Fig. 46. Construction of Skyline, Stage 3. Vertical Scale: $9° = \cdot 1$ in. All horizontal angles are measured from Vc (Fig. 45). To verify, compare this result with a view of Harrow Hill from Preston. Horizontal Scale: $1° = \cdot 1$ in. Owing to want of space, only the sector dce (Fig. 44) is included.

The skyline, or furthest background, having been determined, the features of the middle and foreground can then be filled in. These too can be inserted by the drawing method given above.

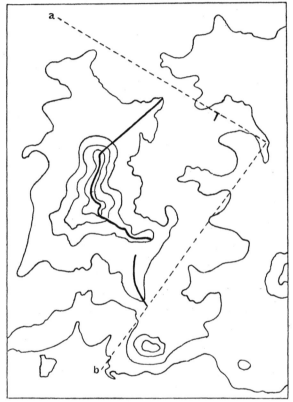

Fig. 47. Path of Skyline. The thickened line denotes the path. Note the breaks.

With a little practice these nearer features are easily fitted into the background, and thus a complete, if rough, picture of the scenery can be formed. If desirable, the dead ground can be shaded on the map without much further trouble.

Fig. 48 a. Map of Llanberis and Snowdon.

1. Compare the map with the accompanying photograph and identify: the castle, the quarries, Llyn Peris, Snowdon and the viewpoint.
2. Find on the map the bluff shown on the left of the photograph, the two hills in the middle ground, the valley in the left centre, and the peak in the background up the valley.
3. Find the distance from the viewpoint to the castle, to the Llanberis Hotel, and to the summit of Snowdon.
4. Estimate from the photograph the distance from the viewpoint to the summits of the two hills and to the brow of the bluff in the middle ground.
5. The valley in the left centre of the photograph is U-shaped. Can you pick out any characteristics in the photograph, on the map?

Fig. 48 b. Photograph of part of the area shown on the map opposite. Trace on the map the sector within the view and mark the path of the skyline.

It must be emphasised at this point that in the construction of a view, as in all map reading indeed, skill increases in direct proportion to the amount of practice. As soon as the reader can construct his skyline by the drawing method, he should test his accuracy by constructing the skyline as seen from some local point and by comparing his result with the actual skyline. This will bring home the reality of the connexion between the map and the ground; for one of the dangers of confining practice to the house is that map reading is apt to be regarded as a mere intellectual exercise. At a later stage a rough outline of the skyline should be sketched on the ground from the actual viewpoint, and the corresponding line traced on the map. This exercise is especially useful in training the reader to locate the skyline without the drawing method.

Middle and foreground features can be studied in the same way. If a sixth of the horizon is chosen for the sector an adequate number of available views can be obtained from a single point. Those who live in big towns and cannot find good views within convenient distance may practise on panoramic photographs (see Fig. 48 *b*). The viewpoint and skyline of the photograph should be identified first and afterwards the various features, both natural and artificial. To find the viewpoint, decide how far below the central point of the bottom of the photograph the camera lens was; find two or more pairs of points in the view which lie on the same straight line from the lens; identify these pairs of points on the map; draw the rays which pass through them; and the meeting point of the rays is the required viewpoint.

CHAPTER IV

FIELD WORK WITH MAP AND COMPASS

14. The Use of the Map in the Field

So far, the treatment of map reading has been preliminary and as such has been regarded as an indoor subject. It is, of course, better for the learner to compare known features on the ground with their representations on the map and to check his topographical descriptions by a visit to the area. A good deal can be done out of doors in the study of gradients, dead ground and intervisibility, and indeed the learner will never form a realistic idea of these matters unless he carries his theoretical work into the field. But after all, the object of map reading can only be fulfilled out of doors, and the duty of this part of the text will be to enable the learner to use his map in the field and to suggest suitable practice for him.

Setting a Map. The first step is to learn how to *set* the map. Broadly speaking, this means placing the map in such a way that the directions shown on the map coincide with those on the ground. To do this, the map must be so placed that a north-and-south line drawn on it coincides with a meridian on the ground. This can be done in several ways:

(i) When the reader's position is unknown:

(a) Place the map on some straight feature (railway, road, canal, etc.) so that the direction of the representation of the feature on the map coincides with that of the feature on the ground.

(b) If two objects can be identified on both map and ground, place the map so that the direction of a straight line joining the representations of the objects on the map coincides with an imaginary line joining the two objects on the ground. This process is known as 'lining in'.

(c) If you can identify two objects, but cannot place the map on the straight line joining them, turn the map into such a position that the straight lines joining the identified objects on the map with the objects themselves will meet somewhere

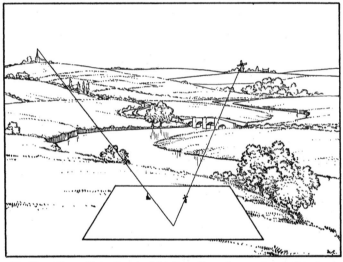

Fig. 49. Resection. Note the straight lines through prominent objects on the ground and their representations on the map in the foreground. The point at which these lines cut each other is the reader's position. A map so placed is *set*.

on the map. See Fig. 49. This can be done accurately with a sight rule and has the advantage of finding one's position on the map. The process is known as *resection*.

(ii) When the reader's position is known:

Identify an object on the ground, and join your position on the map by a straight line to the representation of the object on the map. Using this line as a sighter, turn the map so that the prolongation of the line reaches the object identified.

Identification of Position. Some objects, like churches, wind-mills, cross-roads, monuments, are easily identified on the map or recognised on the ground. They form points from which less well-marked positions, e.g. a spot in an open field, a hillock, etc., may be identified. Thus, a hillock a quarter of a mile from a certain church on a bearing of 25° may be found easily enough. The beginner should train himself to find positions thus described, as the practice is the basis of good map reading in the field. Other objects are continuous (e.g. roads, railways, rivers, canals, etc.) and, though easily identified, are useful for finding positions only in conjunction with other features, as for instance when two roads cross or join each other, when the stream or canal is bridged or fordable, etc.

In the field the map reader is faced with three problems of position:

  (i) Where am I at the start?
  (ii) Where am I *en route*?
  (iii) Where can I find my objective?

The first is easy enough, assuming that the start is made from a spot known to the map reader. He would set out from a village, railway station, or cross-road, which he can identify on both map and ground. But when the starting-point is left behind, it is not always easy for the beginner to identify his position. Suppose that he is moving along a road: then the matter is comparatively simple. He must keep a look out for objects which are easily identified, especially road junctions along his route, and map in hand he should follow carefully his progress along the road. Where the road is straight or some prominent object constantly in view, he is in no difficulty. But on a winding road with tall, thick hedges or trees on both sides, he must check his position whenever an opening gives him an opportunity. When there is no break in the foliage, he should calculate roughly the distance he has travelled along the road and find his approximate position thus. Recognis-able bends and roadside features which are marked on the map will help him to identify his position as he goes along. If he loses his place, he should take the first opportunity of finding it again by resection (see above, section 14 (i) *c*). A little practice will enable him to find his position so easily that constant reference to the map will be unnecessary. By looking ahead on the map and noting what landmarks to expect and when he should see them, he can dispense with the map for long distances, especially when the country is simple.

If he is moving across country, he must identify some distant object on the line he proposes to follow and make for this as directly as possible. Intervening features can be identified either by resection (done roughly by the eye) or by calculating the distance travelled. A simple method which can be used if there is a succession of well-marked features, e.g. low hills, farms, roads, etc., is to take count of the series and judge the position between the nearest two. In open country where the number of recognisable points is few, it is as well to keep constant tally of one's position, identifying the natural features whenever possible. The beginner often feels hopeless over this, but he soon begins to develop a kind of sense of position. A good deal of practice is necessary. Accurate judging of distance is required, for the beginner is prone to overestimate distances on the map and underestimate them on the ground.

When the objective is neared, if it is not an easily recognisable object, some difficulty may arise in its identification. This frequently occurs when the approach has been across country and when the objective is one of several similar underfeatures. The shape of the feature should be carefully examined on the map and any distinguishing mark sought for on the ground. If the position cannot thus be identified with certainty, the 'lie' of various features with respect to each other may give a clue. Failing this, resection may be resorted to. When this is impossible because there is no recognisable feature in sight, it will be necessary to move to some position whence points may be identified.

To make the best use of a map across country or to use one at all at night or in foggy weather, the reader must be provided with a compass of some kind, and the use of this instrument will form the subject of the next section.

<h2 style="text-align:center">15. COMPASS WORK</h2>

Two kinds of compasses are used for map work, pocket and prismatic. The former, of which there are many varieties, are useful for rough work, but, owing to the difficulty in reading them accurately, are of little use when greater precision is required. The latter, of which the standard variety is the Army pattern, allows far greater precision to be attained and should be used whenever possible.

The Compass. Compasses, whether pocket or prismatic, consist of a metal *box* with a hinged *lid*. In the box is a glass *cover*,

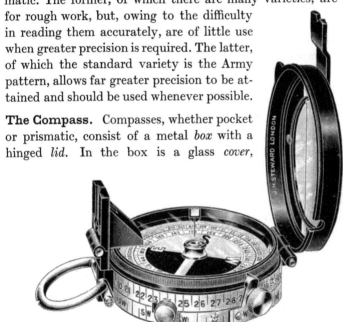

Fig. 50. A Prismatic Compass (military pattern).

beneath which is the dial or *card* with the *needle* attached underneath. The card and needle pivot on a steel point, and the former is divided like a protractor into degrees numbered from 1 to 360. Inside the box there is a vertical line, known as the *lubberline*.

On the outside of the box there is a *stop* which lifts the card off the pivot when the compass is not in use. When the card is released from the stop, it oscillates for some time before coming to rest; hence most compasses are fitted with a *check spring* to shorten the oscillations. The better varieties of prismatic compass are filled with liquid which renders both the stop and the check spring unnecessary.

Prismatic compasses of the Army pattern have in addition a circular glass *window* in the lid, with a *hairline* engraved on it. At each end of the hairline are luminous strips for use at night. There is also a brass ring for holding the compass. The first joint of the thumb should be passed through the ring and the box allowed to rest on the curved index finger. This has been found by experience to be the steadiest way of holding the compass. The lubberline and the hairline when produced pass through the centre of the compass and reach the extremities of the instrument in two notches. One is cut in the brass ring, the other in the *tongue* which forms an extension of the lid. Such a line is known as the line of *notches*.

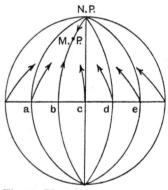

Fig. 51. Theory of Magnetic Variation illustrated. M.P. is the Magnetic Pole, N.P. the North Pole. The meridians converging on the North Pole show the direction of True North. The arrows converging on the Magnetic Pole explain why Magnetic North differs from True North in most places.

The principle of the compass is that its magnetised needle or pointer always points to the north. Once this direction has been identified, the other cardinal points can be found. But the compass needle does not always point towards the North Pole, but towards a point in Boothia Island, which is known as the *Magnetic Pole*. The direction of the North Pole, or *True North*, always runs along a meridian. Fig. 51 shows that of all the

positions *a*, *b*, *c*, *d*, and *e*, the only one at which the direction of the
compass needle coincides with a meridian is *b*. Position *b* is thus
favoured because it is on the same meridian as the Magnetic Pole.
At all the other positions there is some *magnetic variation*, i.e.
deviation of the direction of north as shown by the compass from
the True North. The variation at *a* is eastwards, and at *c*, *d*, and
e it is westwards, increasing with distance from the meridian of
the Magnetic Pole. At places between the North Pole and the
Magnetic Pole the needle points south. The matter is not as simple
as this, but what has been said will give a rough idea of the
general principle of magnetic variation.

The compass, then, points to *Magnetic North* and not necessarily
to *True North*. This is not all, for the magnetic variation changes
as time goes on at any given place. Hence, maps are made to show
True North. To use the map efficiently, the reader must know the
magnetic variation for the time being in the district in which he
is using the map. The one-inch O.S. Popular map contains an
arrow in black pointing to True North and one in outline pointing
to Magnetic North. The variation is given in angular measurement,
and the year for which this variation was correct is noted. The
annual rate of change (not constant) is also given. Compass
readings must be adjusted before being applied to the map.

Taking a Bearing. Direction is found by means of a compass
through angular measurement in the same way in which a protractor is used to measure bearings on a map (see section 3). To
take a bearing hold the compass as explained above, apply the
eye to the *sighting slot*, bring the hairline and the objective in line
through the slot. Then, keeping the compass steady, glance down
through the magnifying prism and read off the number of degrees
from Magnetic North of the objective. This is the *magnetic bearing*.

Adjustment of Magnetic to True Bearings. To adjust a magnetic to true bearing, add or subtract the amount of magnetic
variation for the time being in the district. E.g. if the magnetic

L M R   6

$\dfrac{1}{63,360}$

bearing is 60° at a place in England, subtract 12° 46′ 18″,[1] and get the true bearing 47° 13′ 42″. Fig. 51 shows why places with a variation west give magnetic bearings greater than true bearings by the amount of the magnetic variation, while those with variation east give magnetic bearings smaller than the corresponding true bearings by the amount of the variation. The magnetic variation in the British Isles can be found in *Whitaker's Almanac* for the current year.

Exercises on the Adjustment of Bearings

1. Reduce the following to true bearings (Mag. Var. 14° W.): 14°, 20°, 54°, 129°, 205°, 315°, 333°, 349°, 352°, 358°.

2. Using the same figures as true bearings, find the corresponding magnetic bearings (Mag. Var. as before).

3. If the Magnetic Variation is 13° 16′ W., what is the true bearing for: 25°, 43°, 51° 30′, 64°, 82° 30′, 6°, 10°, 274°, 291°, 330° 30′, 348°, 351° 30′?

4. Using the figures in Question 3 as true bearings, find the corresponding magnetic bearings (Mag. Var. as before).

(References on the following are to Map V)

5. Find the true bearings from A to G, B, and C; and turn them into magnetic bearings (Mag. Var. 14° W.).

6. Find the successive true bearings to T of a person moving from D to H and on to B and to G. Convert these to magnetic bearings, reckoning the Magnetic Variation as 13° 30′ W.

7. A traveller moves due south (Mag.) from A until he reaches a point due east (Mag.) of C. Find his final position (Mag. Var. 14° W.).

8. Trace the route of a traveller who walked from K on a magnetic bearing of 330° (Mag. Var. 12° W.) for 1½ miles, then on a magnetic bearing of 14° for 2 miles, then on a magnetic bearing of 45° for 1½ miles.

9. An observer at B found that K was due south (Mag.) of him. What was the Magnetic Variation of his compass?

10. Wishing to test his compass, a man takes a bearing from A to B. If the Magnetic Variation is 13° 15′ and he finds his compass bearing to be 274°, what does the inaccuracy of his compass amount to?

11. A man moves along a path from C to A and on to P. He checks his position by a landmark at B. What should his true bearing be when he is halfway to A and at A? (Mag. Var. 10° E.).

---

[1] This is the reading for 1928 at Abinger near Dorking in Surrey, to which place the duties of recording earth magnetism have been transferred from Greenwich.

Use of the Compass with the Map. If the map reader is provided with a prismatic compass, he can easily set his map with its help. He should first produce on the map the arrow which points to Magnetic North. This done, he lays the map flat and places the compass on the produced line so that both notches are exactly on the line. He must now turn map and compass together gently (without displacing the compass) until the needle points to the lubberline. The map is then set.

One's position, if unknown, can now be found by resection. Take the bearings of two recognised features or objects, reduce them to true bearings, and lay off these bearings on the map, producing the lines till they meet. The point of intersection of the lines is the required position. This method gives far more accurate results than the sighting involved by resection without the compass. If no landmark can be recognised for certain, move to the top of the nearest eminence or to some other suitable place whence the view will be extended and the possibility of identifying some feature greater.

Having identified one's position, one may use the compass for further identification of surrounding features. Select a feature, take a bearing to it, reduce the magnetic bearing to true, and lay off the bearing on the map. By following the bearing from one's position on the map, the feature can usually be identified. If two similar features, e.g. low hills, lie on the same bearing, the one in sight must be the nearer. It is unnecessary to draw lines on the map: a transparent protractor will show the line without further trouble. This use of the compass is often the only safe way of identifying low or similar hills when several occur close together.

Moving on a Compass Bearing. Moving across country with the aid of a compass is far easier than with the map alone, for the compass enables one to dispense with the identification of features. After learning the magnetic bearing of the proposed route, all one has to do is to take a sight with the compass so that the required bearing comes opposite to the lubberline, then look ahead through the sighting slot and select some distant object on the line of bearing. One now proceeds to the object thus selected and repeats the procedure, until the objective is reached. To reduce possible inaccuracy, the selected landmark should be as distant as possible.

At night, or in foggy weather, special methods must be used. The Army pattern prismatic compass is provided with a glass cover which can be rotated unless held in position by a *clamping screw*. Near the edge of the cover is a luminous *direction mark*. The edge itself is milled, and in non-liquid compasses opposite the centre of the direction mark is an incised line, the *setting vane*. This works on a graduation on the outside of the box. In liquid-filled compasses this graduation is etched on the glass cover and works on the lubberline. There is therefore no setting vane. To *set* the compass, rotate the cover until the setting vane (or, in a liquid-filled compass, the lubberline) corresponds with the required bearing. The compass is now ready for use.

To proceed from one point to another by night, set the compass, open the lid flat, and let the needle come to rest in line with the direction mark. The direction of one's route is now indicated by the luminous patches on the line of notches. In black darkness, and when one is alone, one must follow this direction as best one can, keeping the compass constantly open before one. If there is sufficient light to see objects ahead, it is best to select one on the line of bearing, proceed to it, and then repeat the process until the objective has been reached. A good deal of time can thus be saved. If one is not alone, a companion can be sent ahead along the line of bearing as far as possible. He must then stand still while the compass bearer rejoins him. By repeating this operation the objective can be reached. If the man sent ahead uses a torch, he can be sent on as far as the voice will carry. The greater the distance he goes, the more accurate will be the route. But for military work the showing of a light and the shouting required to get the advanced man into line with the compass bearing have obvious objections. In foggy weather the procedure is the same, though rather easier.

Deflection of the Compass. It must be remembered that iron and some other substances cause the compass needle to be deflected from the direction of Magnetic North. Hence, in using the instrument, one should stand well away from iron fences, metal rails, etc. Motor cars cause very great deflection, and a bearing taken from a car is useless. One should stand at least 20 yds. from a car to be sure that the compass is free from deflection.

16. THE INTERPRETATION OF THE MAP

When the reader can recognise the topography and, piecing together the features, conjure up a mental picture of the scene shown on the map, he has achieved much, as much perhaps as will satisfy the 'practical' man. But if he leaves his progress at that, he is like the man who, having learnt to read and write, confines the use of his acquired skill to business communications and ignores literature entirely. Reading and writing have their practical uses, but from earliest times they have also had the far higher purpose of transmitting, not the passing matter of the moment, but the immortal treasures of the world's store of thought. The art of expressing beautiful thoughts beautifully, of cunningly blending allusion and association, and of faithful description of life and nature has always been one of man's greatest sources of innocent pleasure. Map reading can be raised to such a pitch of art that it produces pleasures not unlike the joys of literature, and it is the aim of the present section to suggest how these pleasures may be gained.

A man, however, cannot be taught to read a map in the fullest sense any more than he can be taught to paint a great picture or to write a great drama. If he wishes to become a great artist, he must learn the rules of the art of drawing; if a great dramatist, the fundamental rules of dramatic composition. So the map reader must learn the principles upon which map symbolism is based. Beyond this no teaching can take him. Suggestions from the ideas of others, lines of thought to be followed up, knowledge of the achievements of fellow-artists—all this may help; but there can be no dogmatism, no laying down of method, no final determination of the goal to be aimed at. Nothing but imagination can help him beyond the mechanical stage.

Map reading differs, however, from all other arts in being entirely individual. There is no picture to be viewed by others, no libretto to be submitted to the judgment of an audience. Whatever the map reader's art produces is for himself alone. This may seem a selfish form of art, but it has the advantage that the poor performer need entertain no feeling of diffidence, since his inferior production will not be inflicted on others. Such virtues as it has will be his pleasure, and that is much. It is a comfort to know that not only the highly talented may aspire to a quota of success. Hear what R. L. Stevenson says: 'I am told there are people who do not care for maps, and find it hard to believe. The names, the shapes of the woodlands, the courses of the roads and rivers, the prehistoric footsteps of man still distinctly traceable up hill and down dale, the mills and the ruins, the ponds and the ferries, perhaps the *Standing Stone* or the *Druidic Circle* on the heath; here is an inexhaustible fund of interest for any man with eyes to see or twopence worth of imagination to understand with.'

A couple of stories may illustrate, *lucus a non lucendo*, the use of the imagination. An American tourist after visiting Westminster Abbey with a friend summed up his impressions with the remark: 'Mighty fine house! Guess it cost a pile of money!' Yet it is not recorded that he was ever troubled by any of the ghosts of the great departed who lie within.

The other tale takes us to Central Africa, where a great railway had just been completed, opening up thousands of miles of country to the world and pregnant with revolution for the lives of the native dwellers. To the opening ceremony the local governor had bidden the high chief of the district. The native watched with keen interest as the beflagged train made its ceremonious passage over the final section of the line. What an occasion, O shade of Cecil Rhodes! The train completed its passage, drew up, and the governor led the chief to inspect the mysterious iron horse. Round the engine walked the chief, his eyes glittering with excitement. At last he stopped, laid a hand on it, and seemed about to make a speech. An expectant audience listened as the words fell from the chieftain's lips: 'Why, it's hot', he said.

If imagination cannot be imparted, it may at least be induced to function, if it exists at all, by being shown paths along which it may work. Three main lines may be suggested: the physical, the human, and the historical. To follow them presupposes a little knowledge of certain subjects such as every educated man does or should possess, or at any rate can acquire without much trouble from a small text-book.

To begin with, the map reader should have some idea of the resistant power and degree of permeability of the rocks of which the country is made, for topographical evolution owes most of its local features to these two qualities in the material on which the forces of erosion work. Without some acquaintance with geology, he cannot comprehend the ultimate causes of, say, the contrasts in the topography of the Sussex Downs and the Cumbrian Mountains or understand why the woodland of Cannock Chase stands isolated among the factory chimneys that surround it.

Given similar conditions of moderate rainfall, running water will carve out V-shaped valleys. Such valleys abound throughout the country. But in the soft, easily eroded chalk of the Downs the angles of the V's tend to be worn off, so that the topography assumes its well-known rounded character. Among the resistant rocks of Cornwall, on the other hand, the angles of the V's are sharp and the smaller re-entrants are almost always gullies. Contrast both of these with the limestone hills of Derbyshire, where the unequal weathering of the rock gives rise to broken ground, caves, enclosed depressions, and a number of other minor features.

The work of rivers affords one of the most interesting episodes in topographical evolution. Each stream has its own territory—its basin—which appears static on the map. But the reader knows that every little blue line of water is engaged in a struggle of life and death with its neighbours. Nor is victory always to the big. Helped by its steep gradient, the little river gradually invades the territory of its larger neighbour and, beheading its enemy, annexes his upper course. The elbow of capture remains for long ages to mark the issue of the struggle. So the Thames lost half its waters to the Severn, so the Ouse has gathered unto itself all the streams of the Vale of York. In every range of hills those who look for it may see this war of streams in every stage. Here a river as it eats its way back must ultimately behead another, but the end is delayed by a massive ridge; there the lowness of the waterparting shows that victory is at hand, as geologists count time.

These are incidents in topographical evolution which the seeing eye can catch and which owe their charm to the interest inspired by all common developments of nature. But our imagination has its allusive as well as its pictorial side and can give us pleasure by recalling episodes of former times and other places. The U-shaped valley seen on the map sheet of the Welsh or Scottish mountains recalls the great Ice Ages when all Scotland and Wales and half of England lay buried, as Greenland does to-day, beneath an immense sheet of ice. The prehistoric cave men, if they yet existed in our islands, were driven south, not to return until after long ages the ice cap melted, soil was again formed on the bare rock, and the vegetable covering which provided food for man's prey grew up once more on the land. Of this episode in the physical history of our country we are also reminded when we see on the map the rounded outline of the hills whose ragged edges were all planed off by the vast mass of slow-moving ice.

By the shores of the south-west coast another force is at work. There dotted on the map are seen the dunes formed of sand blown inshore by the prevailing wind. Unimportant features, it is true; yet they remind us that the fertile land of the south-west of France was once threatened by an ever-advancing tide of sand dunes which were only prevented by the genius of Bremontier from turning the vineyards of Bordeaux into a desert. Or else they may recall to some the grimmer struggles among the sand hills of Belgium when a more pitiless tide of invasion threatened the land of France.

Physical developments explain many of the causes of certain forms of human activity. Here the modern road winds its way among the hills ever compromising between shortness of route and ease of gradient. There the straight course of a Roman road still in use recalls the story of the engineers tracing their path by aligning long rows of legionaries. With their orderliness of mind and the desire to avoid defiles, they drew their paths over hill and dale without deigning to notice mere topography. In other places a ford or a bridge over a river is seen to draw to it the roads which bend out of their straight paths and converge to form a nodal point marked by a town. Romantic are some of the names of these old fords and often tantalising, since their story has long since passed out of memory. Why Hertford? we ask. Did some hunted deer show this crossing to its pursuers, even as a stag betrayed the English to defeat at Pathay? Hereford, the ford of the army, has surely some history connected with its name.

Like the paths followed by routes, the positions of towns have been determined by the physical features. The matter has been dealt with elsewhere, but one or two additional points may be noted. In purely agricultural districts the sites of farms and villages are influenced by three factors: ease of communication and transport, water supply, and central position as regards the cultivated land. The banks of a stream usually fulfil all three conditions, and the number of villages thus situated is remarkable.

In hilly districts the dwellings prefer the lower, less exposed ground, while in plains liable to winter floods they tend to occupy the high ground. Thus, round the north-west of London the old towns and villages noticeably shun the damp clay of the low ground and occupy the tops of rises and hills where the drainage is better owing to the greater slope or to the presence of gravel or sand. The row of villages that frequently skirt the foot of an escarpment or range of hills will be found on examination to stand on the line of contact between a permeable and an impermeable layer of rock. The determining cause of the position of the villages is therefore the presence of springs. Examples of such influence may be seen at the foot of the hills enclosing the Thames valley. On the other hand, in streamless chalk districts the dwellings are forced to occupy the valley-line.

In a country of freemen it might be thought that each individual would be able to choose his own occupation. Yet it is not so. A privileged few may have their choice, but for the many their life's work is decided for them by the topography of their native district. The men of the lowlands of East Anglia are agriculturists, those of the hill country of Sussex, Wales, and Yorkshire are shepherds. They cannot help it. The topography of their district has decided that growing cereals and roots is the most profitable business in East Anglia and that sheep rearing pays best on the well-drained grass slopes of the hills. Geology is not without its influence on occupation, for who can escape the toils of industrial life in the great manufacturing districts which owe their existence to the presence of coal and iron?

Hence it is that density of population is influenced by topography. Do we see on the map a hilly district given up to sheep rearing? Then the density of population is low. Do we see a fertile alluvial plain? Then the density is high. In an industrial area it is highest of all; and lowest where, as in the Scottish Highlands, the hard, almost soilless rock gives a poor return for human labour. Heaths and moorland are scantily peopled, but are often used as 'commons', grouse moors, or deer 'forests'. In modern times the commons of the south of England are increasing in value owing to their use as golf courses.

Not only do the natural features dictate what a man must do and where he must live: they also determine the material of which his house is built. The map reader who pictures the scene in a Dorsetshire sheet will not be far wrong if he imagines the houses to be of grey local stone, while if he is reading a sheet showing the alluvial clay plain of the Thames valley he will surely give the buildings the tone of red brick. In Carnarvonshire dwellings are of local stone roofed with tiles from the neighbouring quarries.

The imagination rises to its greatest height, however, when following out the historical associations suggested by the map. Take a sheet showing Salisbury Plain and look for the little discs marked *tumulus*. Near by perhaps is Sidbury Hill crowned by the inscription 'British Village'. Further west we find holier ground, for there is Stonehenge. All these are the traces of the prehistoric inhabitants of the Plain, men whose villages crowned the moat-encircled hill-tops, who worshipped at a mysterious shrine, and who when dead were buried under mounds so vast as to have survived to this day. One need not be a student of archeology or anthropology to feel the glamour of these old remains.

Elsewhere we find Watling Street or some other old Roman way. We seem to see the legions marching along them, their armour clanking and glittering in the sun; while here and there the inscription 'camp' brings to mind the military nature of their occupation of the country and their constant need to hold strategic points. Watling Street reminds us too of that treaty which ended the epic struggle of the great West Saxon king in defence of his realm. But not all the camps which dot the map are Roman. Some are the handiwork of Alfred's enemies, and, turning up a map sheet at random, we may see for instance the name Dansbury in Essex, which is derived from the neighbouring camp of Danish invaders.

Place names indeed contain an epitome of the country's history. The prominent features (Downs), rivers (Avon, Ouse, etc.), even the city of London itself, keep the names bestowed by the first historical owners of the soil. Great strategic points are marked by the Roman *chester*, while the vast majority of town, village, and forest names are those given by the English settlers. Widely scattered over the north and east of England are the names substituted by Danish or Norse invaders. What is true of England is no less true of Wales and Scotland: the story of former movements of peoples is written large on the map.

Everywhere in England we find in the names of country seats plain evidence of the Norman Conquest and the consequent substitution of William's successful soldiers for the English thanes. Thus, Chequers, Villiers, Mornay's, etc. Occasionally in the north we find castles, like Brancepeth, which recall the terrible years of anarchy under Stephen when 'Christ and his saints slept'. But most of the castles, now usually in a more or less advanced state of ruin, are traces of the picturesque era of medieval chivalry and call up associations of Froissart, Border Ballads, the *Mort d'Arthur*, and a hundred other pleasing things. The Manor or Hall and the Common are survivors of the medieval rural system which was so rudely ended by the ravages of the Black Death.

As we draw nearer to modern times, things lack the interest of antiquity; but here and there we see a house which sheltered Henry VIII or Elizabeth, there a battlefield made famous by some bloody encounter of the Wars of the Roses or the Great Rebellion. That tower standing near the coast is a martello, built when Napoleon's threatened invasion seemed a not impossible calamity. A famous road, like the Bath or the North Road, with its once equally famous inns, now sadly decayed, but somewhat rejuvenated by the flow of motorists, conjures up the old coaching days, and we seem to hear the rattle of wheels and the crack of the postillion's whip. This leads on the train of thought to Dick Turpin and his fellow-highwaymen. And so the flight of imagination soars!

All this may be got from a good map. Surely it is better to read thus rather than to treat the map as an elaborate diagram for the guidance of road passengers or a jigsaw puzzle to be solved by military aspirants! Let us conclude with a passage by the late Mr C. E. Montague:[1]

'The notation once learnt, the map conveys its own import with an immediateness and vivacity comparable with those of the score or poem. Convexities and concavities of ground, the bluff, the defile, the long mounting bulge of a grassy ridge, the snuggling hollow within a mountain shaped like a horse-shoe—all come directly into your presence and offer you the spectacle of their high or low relief with a vivid sensuous sharpness.

'Much enjoyment of these delights can generate in the mind a new power of topographic portraiture, a knack of forming circumstantially correct visions of large patches of the earth's surface. You learn, like a portrait painter, to penetrate by the help of intuitive inference; you get at one thing through another. You see on a good map the course of the Mersey—short, traversing a plain for more than the latter half of its length; but also, in its head streams, the Etherow and the Goyt, crossing rapid successions of contour lines in the Pennine moorlands of Longdendale and the Peak. You guess at once what the temper of such a river must be. For it is a very down-comer pipe, as a builder might say, in its upper course, to drain the steeper side of the much-drenched roof of the Pennine, from Buxton northward to somewhere near Oldham. Clearly a stream to be vexed with extravagant spates, swiftly rising and swiftly subsiding, before at last its pace wears itself out in the fat Cheshire flats, as the rushing and tearing Rhine of Basle slows down in level Holland. Then you examine the Mersey on your map, in the lowland reaches just after it works clear of the hills; and, with a happy inward crow of satisfaction you see, if your map is a thoroughly good one, how the stream is

[1] *The Right Place* (p. 41), a sort of travel book of essays which must delight every geographer. (Quoted by arrangement with Mrs Montague.)

flanked throughout the many miles from Stockport to Sale with enormous flood banks raised to guard the riverain farms from just that termagant fury that you had looked out for.

'Every educated person knows, in a sense, how the surface of England is modelled—how the formative ridge of the Pennine is dropped half-way down the country southwards like the firmer cartilage in the flesh of a widening nose; how the lateral bracket of the Lake hills is attached unsymmetrically to this central framework by the Shap bar, and so on. But few such persons conceive it with any imaginative energy or with the delight that such energy brings. The rest have the kind of knowledge that lies dead in the mind, as a classical education lies dead in the minds of most of those who have had it. It has to be raised from the dead by some evocatory miracle of appeal to the sensuous imagination—the kind of imagination that rejoices to take up and carry on the work of a bodily sense at a point where bodily sense can go no further. The work is carried on, at the best, with so much of the eager immediacy of actual sight or hearing, and so little of the dusty cloudiness of common abstract thought, that on a peak of the Alps you may obtain a sensation almost indistinguishable from seeing with the bodily eye the whole structure of the Apennines, the Lombard plain and the silted Venetian lagoon, laid out under your eye. Or from a bulge of high ground in our Midlands, where the Nen, the Welland and the Bristol Avon rise almost together, you may suddenly feel that you see the whole complex of English rivers as sharply clear as you may see the rummaging roots of a bulb grown in a clear glass jar full of water.

> *These delights if you would have,*
> *Come live with me and be my love.*

Thus does the large scale map woo the susceptible mind. Geography, in such a guise, is quite a different muse from the pedantic harridan who used to plague the spirit of youth with lists of chief towns, rivers and lakes, and statistics of leather, hardware, and jute'.

CHAPTER V

OTHER MAPS AND THEIR SPECIAL DEVICES

17. Military Map Reading

The use of the map for military purposes differs in no essential from the ordinary uses. The interpretation of relief, the calculation of relative distance and position, and the deciphering of the conventional signs, all remain the same. But just as in actually viewing a piece of country a soldier's eye sees things in a different light from that of the civilian, so in reading the map the significance of features and other facts has a special value for the soldier. He sees in the trivial kink of a contour a fold in the ground which may be a danger to him in defence or the key to his success in attack. The picturesque defile is to him a feature pregnant with opportunities for an overwhelming surprise. The convex slope is one which offers a poor field of fire, while the concave slope is dominated throughout by an enemy posted on the top. In fact, his eye seeks everywhere the strategic value of the features and regards every district as a potential field of action.

It is naturally the young officer, the platoon commander, who requires the most detailed interpretation of the map, since it is he who must take precautions against or gain advantages from minor features. In an advance along a road, for instance, the danger points should be foreseen. A bend in the road, a cutting, a wood across the path, a defile of any sort—all these afford possibilities of danger which cannot safely be neglected. It is not those dangers which can be seen on the ground that are most to be feared, but those that are hidden and which enable the enemy to effect a surprise. To the map reader equipped with a good map such surprises are impossible. Or, again, in moving across country the advantages of cover offered here and there by dead ground, trees, sunken roads, etc. can be foreseen with the aid of a map and used. The position held by an enemy can be examined and the best approaches to it discovered. Moreover, the enemy's dispositions and possible future movements may be conjectured from the map and counter moves made accordingly. When the view is obstructed by fog, darkness, or the nature of the ground, the direction of march may be preserved correctly and the objective reached, even across country, by the use of map and compass. In defence the map is equally invaluable for the selection of positions and, though nothing can replace personal reconnaissance, yet the commander who can see from his map where dead ground lies and where the dominating positions are will be saved a great deal of time and trouble that may be more profitably expended elsewhere.

In position warfare the accurate use of the map is even more imperative in some respects, and cooperation between artillery and infantry is impossible without proficiency in map reading. This cooperation is so important even in war of movement that topographical maps are specially modified for the purpose, as will be explained in the next section.

18. Gridded Maps

The use of the map for identifying exact position is very important in military matters. The determination of one's own position on the map has already been dealt with. But it is equally important to be able to indicate a given spot with perfect accuracy to some-one who is some distance away and with whom communication is restricted. Conversely, the indication so given must be perfectly understood and the spot accurately identified.

In order to facilitate the indication of position, army maps are gridded, i.e. the whole area of operations is covered with squares like those on the O.S. one-inch Popular map. There is this difference, however, that the squares on the O.S. map are independent on each sheet, while the army grids continue from one sheet to the other. The grid is constructed by choosing a point of origin and drawing through it north-and-south and east-and-west lines. Other lines are drawn parallel to these axes and at a certain distance apart (1000 yds. on old maps, 1 km. on the new). Every tenth line, reckoning from the point of origin, is thickened. Thus the map is divided into large squares with sides of 10 km. (or 10,000 yds.) and into smaller squares of 1 km. (1000 yds.) to the side.

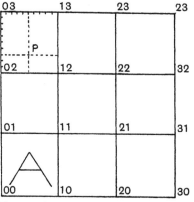

Fig. 52. Grid Method of Map Reference.

The large squares are denoted by capital letters in alphabetical order, the small squares by figures which have no numerical relation with each other. Thus, square A has its letter-name in the south-west corner (Fig. 52). From the south-west point the north-and-south grid lines are numbered eastwards from 0 to 9 and the east-and-west lines northwards from 0 to 9. To indicate a point at which two such lines cut each other, name the east-and-west line first, then the north-and-south. E.g. 00 is the south-west point, the next point along the line eastwards is 10, the next 20, and so on. Along the north-and-south line the second point is 01, the next 02, and so on. Point 11 lies where the second north-and-south line cuts the second east-and-west.

The further subdivision of the small squares is imagined and the tenths thus obtained are added as decimals to the other figures. Thus, in Fig. 52 the point of intersection of the dotted lines is read 0·5—2·3. The letter is also added, so that the full reading is A0·5—2·3. This is known as a *four-figure coordinate*. As soon as the principle is understood it will be seen that by subdividing the squares into hundredths a clear indication will be obtained by means of six-figure coordinates. This kind of *map reference* is especially useful for directing the fire of artillery.

Exercises on Military Map Reading

(*References are to* Map III)

General Situation. Midland and Southland are at war. Southland has mobilised earlier than Midland and intends to invade the enemy's territory through the gaps in the Chilterns. These hills are just within the Midland borders and are held by small forces.

One column of the Southland forces has been ordered to advance through the Wendover Gap, secure the pass, and threaten Aylesbury.

On the evening of June 20 the advanced troops of this column have reached The Abbey (C3), and the outposts of a strong flank guard are at Hanger Farm (C2). No resistance has been met with, though hostile scouts and parties have been seen.

1. What topographical features on the west of the Great Missenden-Wendover road have led to the detachment of a strong flank guard?

2. Describe the country immediately in view of sentries posted (*a*) at the road junction just north-west of the second n of Denner Hill, and (*b*) at White House. Outline in pencil on the map the foreground area in view of each.

3. Can the sentry at White House see (*a*) Great Missenden station, (*b*) The Abbey (C3—54), and (*c*) Hill House (C3—55)? (N.B. Assume the height of trees to be 40 ft.)

4. By what line would a platoon post at Prestwood Lodge get into touch with another post at Nag's Head? What instructions would you give a runner to enable him to find his way to Nag's Head?

Narrative. On the morning of June 21 the Southland troops resume their march. The O.C. flank guard has detailed your battalion to form an advanced guard and decides to move along the road Honorend Farm—Little Hampden—Scrubs—Coombe Hill.

5. You are in command of the vanguard platoon of your battalion. Describe from the map the nature of the country over which you will be operating during the advance to Coombe Hill.

6. Draw a rough sketch of the view before you as you stand at Honorend Farm and look towards Little Hampden. What obstacles close in your view to left and right?

7. On reaching the road junction at C2—38 your platoon is fired on and your further advance lies straight from the road junction to the south-west corner of the wood west of trigonometrical point 603. What is the bearing of your advance? What is the bearing of Great Missenden station from the trigonometrical point? Are the two points intervisible?

8. The ammunition transport wagon has reached the road junction south of Cockshoots Wood. Will the gradient allow it to reach the inn on Little Hampden Common along the course of the footpath shown on the map?

9. Your advance is held up at Little Hampden Common by machine-gun fire and you ask for artillery support. Choose any two suitable spots as the positions of the machine-guns and describe the positions as accurately as you can by means of (a) coordinates, (b) any other system you please.

10. After much fighting Coombe Hill is reached. Describe the ground immediately ahead. What difficulties will the transport wagon meet in advancing further? How can they be overcome?

19. The Use of Other Maps

Besides the one-inch Popular, the Ordnance Survey issues maps on the same scale which differ from our familiar map in various ways, but which do not present any difficulty to the reader of the Popular. Some issues have smaller and other larger scales than the Popular. Of the smaller scales the half-inch and quarter-inch maps may be used topographically, though they do not show minor features. They are especially useful as road maps, for which purpose there is indeed a special half-inch map indicating routes by the new system of numbering devised by the Ministry of Transport. The maps of larger scale are the 25-inch and the six-inch. The former is mainly of use to engineers, surveyors, and property owners. The latter is topographical in that it shows relief as well as other features, but the area on a sheet is too small for ordinary topographical purposes. If, however, one is working on a small area, the six-inch map is the best, as it gives greater detail than the one-inch.

In using these maps the reader of the Popular will find himself somewhat at sea at first, since in them distances and vertical intervals differ from those of his accustomed map. However, a very little practice will enable him to adjust his ideas. But to do this he must consider the question of scales.

Scales. The scale of a map is the ratio between a given distance on the ground and its representative distance on the map. Thus, on the Popular map, 1 in. represents 1 mile on the ground. On the quarter-inch map, $\frac{1}{4}$ in. represents 1 mile, i.e. 1 in. represents 4 miles. The scale is said to be smaller than that of the one-inch because a given length on the ground is represented in it by a shorter distance on the map. On the other hand, the six-inch map has a larger scale than the one-inch, for on it 6 in. represent 1 mile, i.e. 1 in. represents $\frac{1}{6}$ mile (or 293 yds. 1 ft.).

The terms 'one-inch map', 'six-inch map', etc. are merely colloquial, the full expressions being:

one-inch map = map on a scale of 1 in. to 1 statute mile;

six-inch map = map on a scale of 6 in. to 1 statute mile;

ten-mile map = map on a scale of 1 in. to 10 statute miles; etc.

The scale of a map is often expressed as a fraction in which a certain distance on the map is taken as unity and expressed as the numerator, while the corresponding distance on the ground forms the denominator. In converting a word-statement of the scale into a fraction, both the numerator and the denominator should be expressed in the same measure. Thus, a scale of 1 in. to 1 mile may be expressed as $\frac{1}{63,360}$. This means that 1 in. on the map represents 63,360 in. (1 mile) on the ground. The fraction expressing the scale of a map is known as the *representative fraction* and is usually written in the form 1/63,360. The fractional expression of a scale is more convenient than the statement in words, since it permits the use of any measure, whether miles, kilometres, versts, etc. Thus, a scale of 1/100,000 is equivalent to 1 in./100,000 in. (1·58 miles); or to 1 cm./100,000 cm. (1 km.).

A *line scale* is usually drawn on the margin of maps to assist the eye in judging distances and to facilitate the measurement of distances. Military protractors also show various common scales for use when there is no line scale on the map. Failing both these aids, a line scale may be drawn. If the scale of the map is 1/100,000, then 100,000 miles are represented by 1 mile (63,360 in.); therefore, 1 mile is represented by $\frac{63,360}{100,000}$ in. or ·6336 in. The length of the line scale should as a rule be about 6 in. Now, as 1 mile is represented by ·6336 in., 10 miles will be represented by 10 × ·6336 in. = 6·336 in. This length is near enough to 6 in. to be chosen for the line scale. Draw a line 6·336 in. long. Divide it into ten equal parts, each of which will represent a mile. These divisions are known as *primary divisions*. Subdivide the primaries into two, four, and eight equal parts to represent half-miles, quarter-miles, and furlongs. The scale is then complete.

Such a line scale is known as *fully divided* and is unusual. Maps, e.g. the O.S. one-inch Popular, are as a rule provided with an *open divided* scale, i.e. one in which the subdivisions are confined to an extension on the left of the zero.

It is often convenient to divide the line scale so as to show yards instead of half-miles, etc. This may be done as follows: assuming the scale of the map to be 1/63,360, and remembering that the line scale should be about 6 in. long, we argue that, since 1760 yds. are represented by 1 in., 10,000 yds. will be represented by

$$\frac{1 \times 10,000}{1760} \text{ in.} = 5·68 \text{ in.}$$

Draw a line 5·68 in. long and divide it into ten equal parts, each of which will then represent 1000 yds. Number the primaries so that the extreme left is 1, the next on the right 0, the next 1, the next 2, and so on up to 9. Subdivide the left-hand primary into ten equal parts, each of which will represent 100 yds. The scale is open divided and is now complete (see Fig. 53).

Exercises on Scales

1. The scale of the old General Staff map of France is 1/80,000. Construct a line scale showing kilometres and hundreds of metres for use with a sheet of this map.

2. Draw a line scale for use with the old General Staff map of France, showing miles, half-miles, and quarter-miles.

3. The new General Staff map of France is on a scale of 1/50,000. Draw a line scale for use with this map, showing kilometres and hundreds of metres.

4. Construct a line scale for the new French General Staff map, showing miles, half-miles, quarter-miles, and furlongs.

5. Make a line scale for use with an O.S. quarter-inch map, showing miles, half-miles, and quarter-miles.

6. Draw a line scale for use with the 1/200,000 map of France, showing kilometres, half-kilometres, and quarter-kilometres.

7. Construct a line scale for the map in the previous question, showing miles and quarter-miles.

8. Construct a line scale for the O.S. six-inch map, dividing the left-hand primary to show distances of 25 yds.

9. The official map of Iceland is on a scale of 1/50,000. Draw a line scale showing hundreds of yards.

10. A class used a scale of 1 cm. = 100 links in plotting a field survey. Taking 1 metre as the equivalent of 3·28 ft., construct line scales showing (*a*) links and chains, (*b*) hundreds of yards in the primary divisions and tens of yards in the subdivisions.

The effect of a reduction in scale of a map is to simplify the representation of features. Small bends in roads, etc. are straightened out, minor indentations in contour lines disappear, and small objects become too minute to be shown. Besides, much detail has to be omitted in order to prevent overcrowding. Thus, on the reduced scale only the main street of a village may be shown, and to prevent the obscurity of facts shown the V.I. has to be increased so

Fig. 53. Scale of yards for a one-inch map. R.F. 1 : 63,360.

Thousands of yards

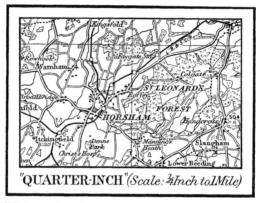

"QUARTER-INCH" (Scale: ¼Inch to 1Mile)

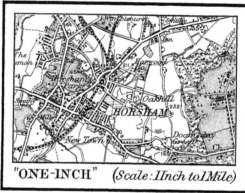

"ONE-INCH" (Scale: 1Inch to 1Mile)

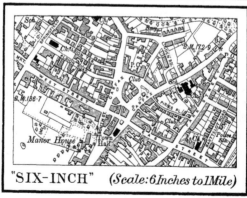

"SIX-INCH" (Scale: 6Inches to 1Mile)

Map VI. A district shown on small and large scales.

Note (i) the amount of detail shown increases with the scale,
        (ii) but the area shown decreases.

as to avoid the overcloseness of the contour lines. Hence, a small scale shows generalisations only (see Map VI). Although this may render the map useless to the topographer, it may be extremely useful for giving a clear idea of the main features of a country. The new O.S. ten-mile map well illustrates this. Whenever the topographical detail is of no great importance, e.g. to the motorist, the simplification of the small scale may be an advantage in itself, not to mention the importance of the inclusion of a greater area on a single sheet. This is what gives the quarter-inch map its advantage over the larger scales in certain circumstances.

In order to become familiar with the representation of relief on a new map, one should draw a scale of standard slopes by one of the methods explained in section 10. If this scale is placed in the margin of the map and referred to whenever gradient is in question, no mistake will be made, and the reader will soon become accustomed to the new scale.

Other Devices for Showing Relief. Contouring is not the only device for showing relief, however, and the reader should make himself acquainted with three other systems. These are all very simple, their only difficulty being that they are likely to mislead, since they belong to the artistic rather than to the scientific side of map making. To take them in historical order, the first is *hill shading* and is derived from the early attempts of map makers to show relief by drawing shaded pictures of hills. To get the effect of light and shade, the light is assumed to come from the northwest and thus all slopes, except those facing the light, are more or less shaded. Flat ground remains unshaded. The obvious drawbacks of the device are that it does not give the shapes of features or any idea of their relative height, while in hilly districts it tends to obscure detail. It gives a good general idea of relief, however, and is fairly satisfactory in small scale maps. Hence, it has been used by the O.S. in a 1/M map, and in older editions of the half-inch and ten-mile maps.

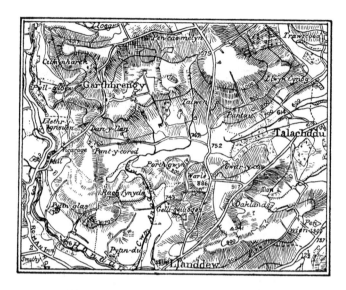

Map VII *a*. Use of hachures to show relief.

A portion of an obsolete O.S. one-inch map.

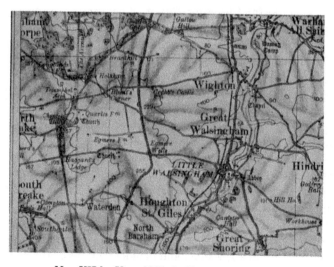

Map VII *b*. Use of hill shading to show relief.
O.S. $\frac{1}{2}$ in. to 1 in.; a portion of Sheet 19.

To remedy the faults of hill shading, the system of *hachuring* was invented. It is merely a conventional form of hill shading in which lines are run straight down the slopes. As before, flat ground is unshaded. The hachures are drawn closer together and thickened to denote increase of gradient. But the system retains all the faults of hill shading, though it has them to a less degree. To realise the inferiority of hill shading and hachures as compared with contours, one has only to try to draw sections from maps in which these systems alone are used. The old General Staff map of France (scale 1/80,000) is a good example of hachuring used by itself.

Hill shading and hachuring, though becoming obsolete, are still used to supplement contours. E.g. the O.S. half-inch Coloured Edition and the new French General Staff map.

The third system of showing relief is *colour layering*. This consists of laying flat bands of colour between given contours. Lower ground is tinted green and higher ground brown, with different shades of the two colours for different heights, so that the colour scale rises from dark green through lighter greens and light browns to dark brown. It is evident that the device can only be used in conjunction with contours. Its faults are that it tends to obscure detail in high ground and that it gives a misleading terrace-like appearance to the surface. But it is extremely useful for emphasising general relief. Hence, it is always used in relief maps of large areas in school atlases and maps. The O.S. has used it, with less success than usual, in the half-inch Layered Edition and with complete success in the quarter-inch New Series Edition and the new ten-mile map. In conjunction with contours, hachures, and hill shading, the device has produced in the one-inch Tourist Edition of the Trossachs what is probably the most artistic work of the O.S.

Foreign Maps. Most countries of Europe have compiled topographical maps on scales varying from 1/25,000 to 1/100,000. Many of them are contoured and most use some additional system of showing relief. The V.I. varies from 2·5 metres to 100 metres. They are to be obtained from official sources. The reader of English O.S. maps will quickly make himself familiar with any of them, but before actual use it is as well to study the conventional signs and other details which differ from those of the English system.

In Asia, Africa, and America, only countries or districts here and there have been thoroughly mapped. India possesses the best maps out of Europe, but Egypt, Turkey, Japan, and the eastern United States are fairly well mapped. No reliance can be placed on maps of other areas.

Revision Exercises, II

1. What is the Ordnance Survey? When was it established?
2. How often is the O.S. one-inch Popular map revised?
3. What information is given in the margin of the Popular map?
4. Explain the use of map squares. How far may the system be carried?
5. What are the bearings of Wendover, Lee, Dunsmore, and Prestwood from Great Missenden Church? (See Map III.)
6. What is the meaning of the little triangle on Coombe Hill?
7. What is a spot height? On what system do you think the points whose heights are specified are chosen?
8. Are the woods on Baddington and Coombe Hills composed of coniferous or deciduous trees, or both?
9. In Map III name by giving end references (*a*) all main roads fit for fast traffic, (*b*) three other roads fit for ordinary traffic, (*c*) two indifferent roads, and (*d*) one minor road.

---

10. What are the parts of a hill? a valley?
11. Define *knoll, crag, col, corrie, gap, outlier, alluvial fan, plateau, gully, catchment basin.*
12. What are the chief topographical lines? Explain their importance.
13. Explain the principle on which contour lines are drawn.
14. On the accompanying diagram (Fig. 54) the height of various points is given. Trace the contours for 50, 100, and 150 ft.
15. With the help of the heights given on the accompanying diagram (Fig. 55), draw contours at intervals of 50 ft. Insert the river.

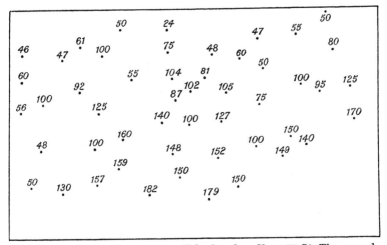

Fig. 54. See Q. 14. The solution will be found on Sheet 57 C6. The ground includes Burnham Thorpe, at the rectory of which Nelson was born.

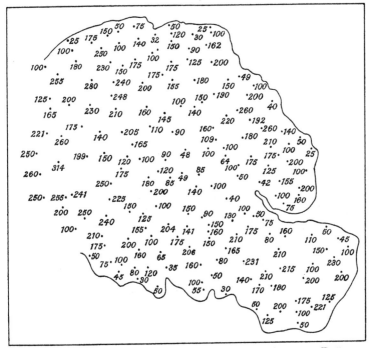

Fig. 55. See Q. 15. The solution will be found on Sheet 146 D15.

16. Fig. 56 shows the course of a stream and its tributaries. Draw approximately the contours for 50, 100, and 150 ft.

17. On Fig. 57 draw the contours for 50, 100, 150, 200, 250, 300, and 350 ft. as indicated by the course of the streams.

18. Draw a section across Map III from Potter Row (C3) to Beacon-hill Farm (A2).

19. On Map III draw a section from Manor Farm (B2—32) to the inn at Lee Gate (B3—46). Mark the position of the railway on the section.

20. Draw a map to represent the area shown in Fig. 15, representing height by contours.

21. Draw contour systems showing a U-shaped valley, an escarpment, a pass, a ravine, and a spur.

22. 'The closer together the contours the steeper the slope'. Discuss the accuracy of this statement.

23. What directions would you give (a) a pedestrian, (b) a motorist, who asked the way from the inn at Prestwood to Dunsmore (Map III)?

24. What two conflicting factors influence the course of roads? Why did the Romans ignore one of them?

25. Wheat is not grown in England above the level of 600 ft. Make a tracing of the 600 ft. contour in Map III and shade the area in which the cereal might be grown.

26. Discuss the origin of U-shaped valleys. Why do they usually begin in a *cirque*?

27. Make a tabular list of dwellings in Map III to show where the influence on position has been mainly due to (a) routes, (b) water supply, (c) central position as regards the cultivated land.

28. Can you account for the general absence of windmills from the area shown in Map III?

---

29. Draw a section from Smalldean Farm (Map III, B2) to Brun Grange (B3). Find the steepest slope in this section and calculate its gradient. Could a cyclist ride, or a horse-drawn vehicle or a motor-car go, direct from the farm to the grange if a straight road existed?

30. What are the standard slopes? What are the corresponding gradients? What useful knowledge have you about each?

31. Construct a gradient scale for use with a map whose horizontal scale is 10 in. to 1 mile and whose vertical interval is 100 ft.

32. Mark on Map III the position of a road unsuitable for a heavily laden lorry.

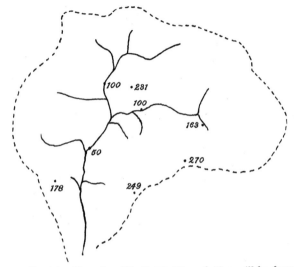

Fig. 56. Revision Exercises II. Q. 16. The solution will be found on Sheet 146 G12. The broken line is a ridge line.

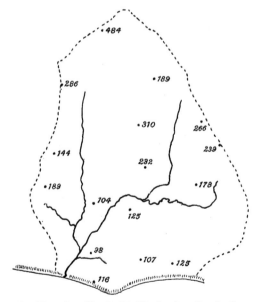

Fig. 57. Revision Exercises II. Q. 17. The broken line is the waterparting. The solution will be found on Sheet 142 H8.

33. Find by inspection whether the following pairs of points on Map III are intervisible: west corner of Halton Wood and World's End (A2—39), the inn at Lee Gate (B3—46) and Durham Farm, Potter Row and Mobwell Inn (C3—26), Concord (B3—19) and Smalldean Farm.

34. Woodlands Park (Map III, B3—31) is not visible from Hunts-green Farm. Find at what point along the road from the park to the farm a pedestrian would come into the view of an observer at the latter place.

35. Is any part of Baddington Hill (Map III, A2—95) visible from Great Missenden Station? Show how you arrive at your answer.

36. At what vertical height must a kite be flown at Hampden Bottom (Map III, C2) to become visible at Woodlands Park?

37. Using your atlas map of England, draw a road section from London to Eastbourne.

38. Draw a section from your atlas map of the L.M.S. Railway route from Leeds via Carlisle to Edinburgh.

39. Construct the view seen from the H of Baddington Hill (Map III, A2—95) within a sector whose bounding rays pass through Wendover Station and Concord respectively.

40. In Map III trace off the contours within the triangle Beaconhill Farm—Wendover Station—Milesfield, and shade all the ground which is dead to an observer at Beaconhill Farm.

---

41. What is meant by 'setting' a map? Explain how you would set your map with and without the aid of a compass.

42. To locate his position on the map a scout takes bearings with his compass. The bearing to the monument on Coombe Hill (Map III, A1—91) is 213°, and to Concord House (B3—19) 134°. Mark his position on the map. (Mag. Var. 12° W.)

43. You are standing on a *tumulus* and can identify a distant church spire on ground and map. How would you proceed to set your map?

44. You are crossing a broad moorland and wish to locate your position on the map. You can identify a distant bridge and a church tower. How would you proceed?

45. An observer at Concord finds the compass bearing of Wendover Church to be 324°. What is the Magnetic Variation of his compass?

46. An observer wishes to find the distance 'as the crow flies' from Kingsash (Map III, B3) to Little London. He takes the bearing of the latter village from Kingsash. Then he paces a distance of 500 yds. along a straight road towards Concord, and then again takes the bearing of

Little London. Assuming that the Magnetic Variation is 12½°, what is the required distance?

47. Explain how you would set a prismatic compass of military pattern for use on a night march.

48. What common features of an English landscape may be regarded as easily identified on map and ground and so used as landmarks?

---

49. How does the date of a Popular map affect the accuracy of (a) woods shown, (b) the amount of Magnetic Variation given?

50. What is a grid? a four-figure coordinate? For what purpose are they used?

51. What is meant by a topographical map? a cadastral map? Name examples of each.

52. Under what circumstances would you prefer a six-inch to a one-inch map? Why?

53. You are about to buy a road map for use in your car. Discuss the claims of the O.S. half-inch, quarter-inch, and ten-mile maps, and say which you finally choose.

54. What various methods are used to show relief on maps? Discuss the advantages and disadvantages of each system.

55. Trace off the contours you drew in answer to Question 15 and shade the map to show up the relief.

56. Do the same again, but show relief by hachures.

57. Trace the contours as before and show up the relief by colour layers.

58. In the defence of Wendover Gap (Map III) against an enemy advancing along the road from the south-east, a company has been allotted the spur from Rignall (C2) north-eastwards to the main road at the 32nd mile. Trace off the contours and mark on your tracing (a) the disposition of platoons by the company commander, (b) and that of the left platoon by its commander.

---

59. Why is Halton (Map III, A2—87, not marked on map) a suitable place for an Air Force camp?

60. What would you deduce from the fact that the majority of place names in Map III are derived from trees, wild animals and birds?

61. Sketch a river basin and its streams, insert towns and villages, and explain your selection of the position of each.

62. What difficulties arise in a limestone area over the water supply?

63. Why are dwellings usually placed on the lower ground in hilly districts and on the higher ground in plains?

64. To what extent does topography influence occupation?

65. How may density of population be read from a map?

66. What influence has geology on local types of dwellings?

67. Why did the prehistoric inhabitants of Britain dwell on hill tops and other high ground?

68. What traces of Scandinavian inroads remain on the map of England?

69. 'All traces of medieval life are not shown on the map as monuments of antiquity'. Enlarge on this.

70. Contrast the use made of moorland by the prehistoric and the modern inhabitants of Britain.

INDEX

Topographical terms are printed in italics

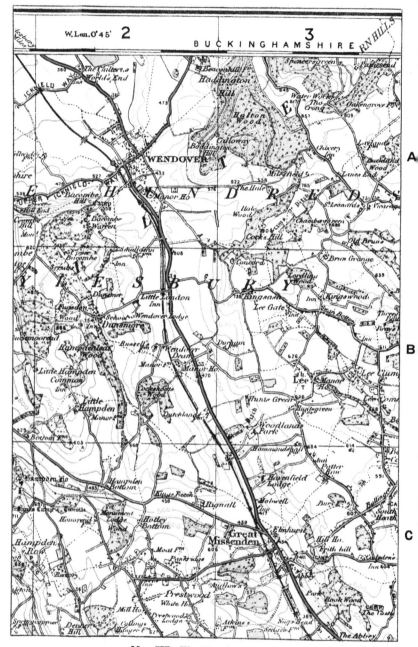

Map III. The Wendover Gap.

(Part of O.S. Popular map, Sheet 106.)

Reproduced from the Ordnance Survey Map with the sanction of H.M. Stationery Office.

For EU product safety concerns, contact us at Calle de José Abascal, 56–1°,
28003 Madrid, Spain or eugpsr@cambridge.org.

www.ingramcontent.com/pod-product-compliance
Ingram Content Group UK Ltd.
Pitfield, Milton Keynes, MK11 3LW, UK
UKHW020307140625
459647UK00014B/1787